Business Best

AF868869

The Business Money Book

Cash, Credit & Collections

by
Jeannette Cloud, CBF

Encouragement Press

Information to Encourage Achievement

1261 West Glenlake
Chicago, IL 60660
www.encouragementpress.com

All rights reserved. No part of this book may be reproduced in any form or by any electronic or mechanical means including information storage and retrieval systems or transmitted in whole or in part, in any form or by any means, electronic, mechanical, photocopying, recording or otherwise–except in the case of brief quotations embodied in critical articles or reviews–without prior written permission of Encouragement Press, LLC, Chicago, IL.

Purchasers of this book are granted a license to use the forms contained in this book for their own personal use. No claim of copyright is made to any official government forms reproduced for the benefit or convenience of the reader.

This publication is designed to provide accurate and authoritative information in regard to the subject matter covered. It is sold with the understanding that the publisher is not engaged in rendering legal, accounting or other professional service. If legal advice or other expert assistance is required, the services of a competent professional person should be sought.

From a Declaration of Principles Jointly Adopted by a Committee of the American Bar Association and a Committee of Publishers and Associations.

ISBN-13: 978-1-933766-18-8 ISBN-10: 1-933766-18-2

This product is not intended to provide legal or financial advice or substitute for the advice of an attorney or advisor.

10 9 8 7 6 5 4 3 2 1

©2007 National Institute of Business Management
1750 Old Meadow Road
McClean, VA 22102
www.nibm.net

Introduction, Resources, Index and Appendices
©2007 Encouragement Press, LLC
1261 W. Glenlake
Chicago, IL 60660
www.encouragementpress.com

Special discounts on bulk quantities of Encouragement Press books and products are available to corporations, professional associations and other organizations. For details, contact our Special Sales Department at 1.253.303.0033.

Business Best

The Business Money Book

Cash, Credit & Collections

About the Author

What does it take to write the book on credit, collections and cash flow? It takes a dedicated author and a woman–Jeannette Cloud, CBF–with 25 years of hands-on experience in credit and collections management (both public and private companies) to explain clearly and precisely why cash flow is so important and how to set up a credit and collection system, no matter how large your company.

Ms. Cloud earned her CBF (Credit Business Fellow) accreditation from the National Association of Credit Mangers and is currently Credit Manager at a major holding company serving the hospitality, food service and consumer markets.

Table of Contents

Introduction

No matter how large or how small your business, the most important factor to ensure its ultimate success and viability is positive cash flow. Literally, cash is king. You may have an exciting product line, you may have the best technology, you may have a great team, but unless you have the fuel–cash–that makes it all work, your business is in trouble. Paper profits may look good but it is cash that will keep you in business.

> According to the Small Business Administration (SBA), nearly 80 percent of new businesses fail within the first 3 years. Frequently a new business is good for a year or two–suddenly it runs out of ideas, customers, vendors and most importantly it runs out of money. Many businesses are undercapitalized from the start; many more do not manage cash flow and expenses properly because they never learned how to do so correctly.

Managing cash flow is taking care of the basics of your business–whether you sell products or services, are for-profit or not-for-profit. It is not complicated nor is it steeped in mystery. You do not need sophisticated accounts receivable and accounts payable programs nor do you need to be a financial genius to do some short-term cash planning. What you do need is a clear understanding of the principles of cash flow, credit and collections–which is what this book is all about.

Do remember that every business is vulnerable, no matter how long they have been in business. The economic climate changes, a big contract is lost, products and technology become obsolete or key employees leave. But you can weather these storms if you anticipate them and plan for major changes.

As the owner/manager you must be absolutely resolute in your determination to maintain and build your cash reserves, using every resource and every program available to you. Pay out as little cash as possible and as late as possible and take in cash as early as possible. Simply put, you need to learn:

- How to make everyday decisions to improve cash management.
- The importance of updating your cash management program.
- The value of the six C's of credit.
- How to improve your collection process.
- Why you should give customers incentives to pay.
- The proper use of collection calls and letters to get paid quickly.
- How to get the entire team involved in cash and collections.

You do not need to hire consultants or send your collection efforts out of the office; instead use the practical, useful and simple advice provided in *The Business Money Book*. Please remember that it does you no good to change your procedures one month and then fall back into old habits. Cash flow, credit and collections need constant vigilance and careful attention.

Learn to survive, even thrive with cash in the bank!

Jeannette Cloud, CBF

Part I

The Essentials of Cash Management

1 Managing Cash Flow

Nothing shapes the health of your company more than cash flow. As the saying goes:

"Profits are an opinion, but cash is a fact."

All managers are aware that profits lend themselves to being managed during any one specific reporting period. There are any number of accounting tactics that can be used to achieve desired corporate or shareholder results. By contrast, your cash flow–or lack of it–is an undeniable reality in business.

The real aim of cash management is to ensure that the right amount of cash is available at the right time to meet your company's needs and objectives. With an effective cash management program, your company will neither be surprised by a developing cash shortage nor find itself stuck with excess cash that should be put to work.

A negative cash flow is not necessarily bad if it is planned as an opportunity cost directed to yielding greater benefits in a foreseeable period. A cash surplus, conversely, can cause your company almost as many problems as a deficit, even though they are less dire. A cash surplus represents assets that are making no direct contribution to your basic business. Even if these assets are invested wisely in financial investments, the yield may fall short of your company's return on investment. Yet there is little that can be done with short-term cash surpluses except to seek out the best possible yields for them, a subject we will discuss later in greater detail.

The problem of imbalances notwithstanding, cash flow is manageable in most respects. You need not accept periodic cash emergencies as inevitable merely because they are common to your industry or have cropped up regularly in the past. There are any number of steps you can take to alleviate cash flow problems, surplus or deficit, or even eliminate them altogether.

Making Cash Flow Decisions

You must keep two basic principles in mind: (1) Cash should not flow into and out of your firm indiscriminately; and (2) getting a handle on your cash flow situation must involve not only a subtraction of payables from receivables but a plan for dealing with the time lag between the two. Look at the major decisions you will have to make to adhere to these principles:

Timing Changes

The easiest way to raise or lower your cash flow is to change the tactical pattern in which cash normally flows into and out of your firm over relatively short periods of time–say, 4 to 6 months. You can speed up collections and/or delay cash outflows to ease a cash deficit. Keep in mind, however, that changes in timing merely alter cash flow patterns for limited periods without changing the amount. They should have no impact on the future performance of the firm or on the firm's long-term investment, marketing and growth goals.

Policy Changes

Changes in policy for the sake of handling cash flow imbalances have much longer-term effects than timing changes. Such changes involve a commitment to alter previously planned objectives–in costs of operations, organization or replacement of plant and equipment, marketing and sales and investment in new products or service development.

From an operational point of view, such policy decisions could include raising or lowering inventory levels or an increase or decrease in research and development spending. From a financial standpoint, you could decide to change your policy on dividends or capital investment programs. Of the two, dividend policy is the more flexible.

Policy decisions that alter the future course of your business should not be made lightly. While such decisions are reversible, they can prove very costly. Therefore, they should be limited to those areas most susceptible to quick response.

Volume Changes

Volume changes are strictly operational in nature and always consist of cutbacks to reduce cash deficits. In addition to planned reductions in sales and/or production, you could reduce raw materials and work-in-process inventories.

Irreversible Policy Decisions

In all likelihood, your most difficult cash flow decisions will involve this area. By its very nature, this type of decision changes your firm in a fundamental way.

Irreversible operational decisions almost always center on assets. You might seek to put surplus cash to use by acquiring a company or another product line, or by disposing of a line or division.

Equity financing is preferred under such circumstances because it does not add to your firm's obligations. However, it is not always possible for a firm with a cash deficit to sell additional common or preferred stock. As a result, many companies are forced to raise new capital via the debt route, which means that future cash flow management must take into account the need to meet debt obligations.

Using Your Cash Budget

Before you can come to grips with cash-management problems, you will need two important pieces of information. First, you must find out just how much cash will flow into and out of your firm. Second, you should have an idea when inflows and outflows will occur. A properly prepared cash budget can help you anticipate problems and even suggest possible solutions.

The cash budget is used primarily to spotlight periods of too little or too much cash rather than for continuous control. The former is usually the problem for smaller companies, and a cash budget can be invaluable. By pinpointing probable cash needs by period and amount, you give your company time to obtain extra funds.

Observation

We have used the same data for both the expense and cash budgets. In practice, the two are usually similar but cannot be exactly alike because of the time lag between sales and collections. Moreover, estimates for operating expenses in a cash budget are usually somewhat more up-to-date.

A cash budget is taken, in large measure, from an expense budget. It starts with a cash balance from the previous year. Then, by using data obtained from the expense budget, it projects the actual ebb and flow of cash transactions for the period.

Where to Get the Right Information

A cash budget can give you valuable information on your probable cash flow trends over a 12-month period. However, to be truly effective in managing your liquid assets, you will need more than guesswork estimates as a guide. You will need information on historical cash flow patterns to judge whether or not your cash budget is realistic. To take timely action to avert potential cash flow problems, you will need information on current cash movements. Finally, to establish an appropriate policy, you will also need to take a look at future cash flow.

Cash flow is quite simple in concept but can be difficult to nail down in practice. The primary problem is that no two firms have exactly the same cash flow pattern. Each company has different critical factors that must be monitored and controlled. Therefore, each firm requires an information-gathering network specifically tailored to its precise needs. This does not mean that you must invent a proprietary methodology for gathering and analyzing cash flow information. Such methodology already exists. We will discuss two broad approaches that provide insights from different points of view.

Receipts & Disbursements Analysis

This is the older and more common method of measuring cash flow. Because it is based on data recorded in the receipts and disbursements log–a basic bookkeeping ledger common to virtually all firms–the information itself is easy to obtain and organize.

Most firms will come up with relatively few general headings for their receipts and payments. Those headings will usually fall into the following categories:

Receipts

There are only a limited number of ways for the average company to obtain cash. It is important, however, that each of those be differentiated in the receipt section of your analysis. Only if each category is identified can you properly monitor your cash receipts, as shown by the following:

Collections

Are funds received from your accounts receivable. Normally, this category will represent the bulk of your cash inflow.

Cash Sales

Sales not involving credit, are usually the next largest category, but they stand far below collections in most companies.

Nonoperating Income

Many companies routinely take in income from sources not necessarily associated with their primary business. This type of income includes dividend or interest income from investments, rental or lease income, royalties and so forth.

Special, Nonrecurrent Sources of Income

The most common items in this category are new financings and the disposal of surplus fixed assets. Income from any unusual source, though, could be included in this category.

Disbursements

There are a number of payment categories that a firm can choose to identify in its analysis of cash flow. Here are some common headings that you might consider:

Supplier Payments

Usually head the list and can consist of cash payments as well as a reduction in accounts payable.

Wages and Salaries

Difficult to control over the short-term, can usually be managed over a period of time.

Overhead Items

Heat, power, telephone, other utilities and property taxes or rent, are generally fixed and beyond management's control. Thus, you can usually bring these items together in one category.

payment categories continue on page 11

Illustration

In condensed form, the expense and cash budgets for ABC Publishing Company appear below and on page 11. Both contain annual and quarterly estimates. Note that the cash budget indicates that ABC will need to borrow $40,000 in the 1st quarter (primarily to pay income taxes) but will be able to pay it back, along with other borrowings, in the 3rd quarter. Moreover, ABC should be able to pay a healthy $50,000 dividend in the 4th quarter and still carry over a reasonable cash balance into the coming year.

ABC Publishing Company Expense Budget

	Full Year	1st Qtr	2nd Qtr	3rd Qtr	4th Qtr
Sales	$600,000	$80,000	$300,000	$150,000	$70,000
Less: Fixed Costs					
Sales	$ 15,000	$ 3,750	$ 3,750	$ 3,750	$ 3,750
Administrative	28,000	7,000	7,000	7,000	7,000
Manufacturing	35,000	8,750	8,750	8,750	8,750
Total Fixed Costs	$ 78,000	$19,500	$ 19,500	$19,500	$19,500
Less: Variable Costs					
Sales	$ 55,000	$ 7,150	$ 27,500	$13,750	$ 6,600
Administrative	12,000	1,560	6,000	3,000	1,440
Manufacturing	230,000	29,900	115,000	57,500	27,600
Total Variable Costs	$297,000	$38,610	$148,500	$74,250	$35,640
Less: Mixed Costs					
Sales	$ 34,000	$ 4,300	$ 17,000	$ 8,500	$ 4,200
Administrative	8,000	1,000	4,000	2,000	1,000
Manufacturing	70,000	9,700	35,000	17,500	7,800
Total Mixed Costs	$112,000	$15,000	$ 56,000	$28,000	$13,000
Income From Operations	$113,000	$ 6,890	$ 76,000	$28,250	$ 1,860
Less: Interest Expense	2,000	–	1,000	–	1,000
Income Taxes	$ 47,460	$ 6,170	$ 23,730	$11,865	$ 5,695
Net Income	$ 63,540	$720	$ 51,270	$16,385	($ 4,835)

ABC Publishing Company Cash Budget					
	Full Year	1st Qtr	2nd Qtr	3rd Qtr	4th Qtr
Beginning Cash Balance	$ 16,000	$ 16,000	$ 11,430	$ 86,430	$ 63,880
Collections	600,000	80,000	300,000	150,000	70,000
Total Available Cash	$616,000	$ 96,000	$311,430	$236,430	$133,880
Less: Cash Payments					
Sales	$104,000	$ 15,200	$ 48,250	$ 26,000	$ 14,550
Administration	48,000	9,560	17,000	12,000	9,440
Manufacturing	335,000	48,350	158,750	83,750	44,150
Total Operating Expense	$487,000	$ 73,110	$224,000	$121,750	$ 68,140
Interest Expense	4,800	–	1,000	2,800	1,000
Income:					
Taxes	$ 47,460	$ 47,460	–	–	–
Dividends	50,000	–	–	–	50,000
Bank Loan Payment	52,000	4,000	–	48,000	–
Cash Balance (Deficit)	$(25,260)	$(28,570)	$ 86,430	$ 63,880	$ 14,740
Bank Borrowing	$ 40,000	$ 40,000	–	–	–
Ending Cash Balance	$ 14,740	$ 11,430	$ 86,430	$ 63,880	$ 14,740

Income Taxes

Can change rapidly and should be classified separately.

Recurrent Payments

Interest on long-term bonds or dividend payments, should be grouped together under a separate heading.

Irregular or Special Financial Obligations

Short-term loan repayments or special dividends, also should be in a separate category.

Capital Expenditures

Can sometimes be significant and, at other times, can amount to no more than a nominal influence on your cash payments. Nevertheless, they should be classified separately whenever possible.

Special Miscellaneous Category

Should be included for extraordinary items (such as the settlement of a lawsuit or a patent purchase) or any other significant, nonrecurring item.

Illustration

To carry on with our previous examples, we have compiled an analysis of receipts and disbursements for the ABC Publishing Company for the 1st quarter of the year, using data contained in the cash and expense budgets for that firm. (See below) Note that the figures for the actual cash flow are consistent, even though the classifications used have been rearranged to suit the format for a receipts & disbursements analysis.

We have confined our analysis to a single quarter, broken down into months. However, there is no need for you to focus on only 1 quarter at a time. If the seasonal patterns for your company warrant, you might choose to consolidate the data semiannually or even annually. But to keep your analysis up-to-date, you will need to compile a new analysis each month.

As the analysis shows, there was advance warning as early as January that cash flow probably would not be sufficient to cover income taxes payable at the end of March. By the end of February, the evidence was conclusive. Hence, with the warning, ABC was able to negotiate a short-term loan that took care of the income tax payment and a modest debt repayment as well.

ABC Publishing Company
Receipts & Disbursements Analysis

	1st Quarter	January	February	March
Receipts				
Collections	$ 62,000	$17,000	$25,000	$ 20,000
Cash Sales	18,000	4,000	5,000	9,000
Miscellaneous	–	–	–	–
Bank Loan	40,000	–	–	40,000
Total Receipts	$120,000	$21,000	$30,000	$ 69,000
Payments				
Suppliers	$ 16,610	$ 3,305	$ 5,105	$ 8,200
Wages & Salaries	34,500	10,500	11,000	13,000
Overhead	22,000	7,000	8,000	7,000
Taxes	47,460	–	–	47,460
Interest & Dividends	–	–	–	–
Debt Repayment	4,000	–	–	4,000
Special Items	–	–	–	–
Total Payments	$124,570	$20,805	$24,105	$ 79,660
Current Surplus (Deficit)	$ (4,570)	$ 195	$ 5,895	$(10,660)
Cash Balance				
Beginning of Period	$ 16,000	$16,000	$16,195	$ 22,090
Cash Balance				
End of Period	$ 11,430	$16,195	$22,090	$ 11,430

Flow-of-Funds Analysis

Analyzing your cash flow by the flow-of-funds method is markedly different from using the receipts & disbursements method. In the latter method, information is organized by account. By contrast, information in a flow-of-funds analysis is organized along the lines of management responsibility. As a result, it will point to the management decision areas that are involved in resolving any cash flow problems that may occur.

Cash Inflow

When viewed along the lines of management responsibility, cash can flow into your company in one of three ways. First, you can receive income from your operations. You also can receive income from a financing, whether it be bank loans, your credit lines or the sale of stock. Finally, you can convert a part of your assets into cash. This can be done by the actual sale of a fixed asset, such as land, a building or machinery. It can also be accomplished by speeding up collection of accounts receivable or selling off inventories.

Cash Outflow

Cash can flow out of your firm in one of three ways when viewed along a management responsibility line.

First, there are normally recurring payments, such as those for taxes, interest payments and dividends. Second, financing obligations may include a loan repayment, bond redemption or perhaps a reduction in your line of credit with suppliers. Finally, you may decide to increase your assets. You could do this by purchasing a fixed asset or by allowing current assets, such as accounts receivable or inventories, to rise.

Once again, note how the end result jibes with both the receipts & disbursements analysis and the cash budget for ABC, even though the information provided by this analysis is entirely different. The cash flow is the same, no matter how it is presented, but there are a number of ways of looking at it.

Even a cursory glance at the flow-of-funds analysis will show that additional financing was necessary to pay the March tax bill. At the same time, a number of other points become apparent as well. First, the seasonal pattern of ABC's operation does not help the company. Even though cash outlays were kept to an absolute minimum in the first 2 months, the modest cash buildup was overwhelmed by out-of-pocket expenses in March. Moreover, even though the slack February period was the proper time to purchase new equipment, ABC would have been hard-pressed to come up with the extra cash if credit had not been available.

You should also note that the flow-of-funds analysis does not give specifics on where the actual cash is being spent, just as the receipts & disbursements analysis makes no mention of management decision areas. Thus, while each method has blind spots, together they can provide you with the information you need to make timely decisions.

Forecasting Your Cash Flow

Either or both of the cash flow analysis methods will go a long way toward satisfying your cash flow information needs. Since both are compiled on a monthly basis, you should be able to track current cash flow patterns easily. In addition, the quarterly consolidations should provide the data necessary to find out whether the assumptions contained in your cash budget were realistic.

Observation

The benefits do not end there. Frequently, a cash flow forecast will help you avoid a costly business mistake or provide an early warning sign that will indicate the path to improved management control. It can also indicate the need to raise significant funds before a crisis or can point the way to proper utilization of an impending surplus.

This leaves one important area to be addressed: the formidable task of forecasting cash flow. Because cash flow is vital to the continued existence of your organization, it is essential that you attempt to predict future cash patterns, if only as a precaution against a possible severe cash squeeze somewhere down the road.

Despite their benefits, cash flow forecasts can cause problems unless you view them in the proper context. Here are some key points to remember:

Completely Accurate Forecasts Are Impossible to Make

No matter how much time and attention you devote to your cash flow forecast, it probably will be wide of the mark. Nevertheless, a properly prepared forecast can yield valuable information by indicating the type of action you should take to avoid cash flow problems.

Forecasts Must Establish Timing

You must attempt to predict not only how much cash will flow into and out of your firm in the future, but also when these flows will occur.

Illustration

To turn once again to our previous example, below you will find a flow-of-funds analysis for ABC Publishing covering the 1st quarter of the year. For demonstration purposes, we have assumed that ABC reduced its inventories during the quarter by $2,000, increased its accounts receivable by the same amount and bought a $10,000 book-binding machine on credit.

ABC Publishing Company Flow-of-Funds Analysis

	1st Quarter	January	February	March
Cash Inflows:				
Income From Operations	$ 6,890	$ 195	$ 5,895	$ 800
Financing				
Bank Financing	40,000	–	–	40,000
New Supplier Credit	10,000	–	10,000	–
Disposal of Assets				
Fixed Assets	–	–	–	–
Current Assets	–	–	–	–
Inventories	2,000	2,000	–	–
Accounts Receivable	–	–	–	–
Total Cash Inflows	$58,890	$ 2,195	$15,895	$ 40,800
Cash Outflows:				
Recurring Payments				
Taxes	$47,460	–	–	$ 47,460
Dividends	–	–	–	–
Interest	–	–	–	–
Financing				
Loan Repayment	4,000	–	–	4,000
Reduced Supplier Credit	–	–	–	–
Acquisition of Assets				
Fixed Assets	10,000	–	10,000	–
Current Assets	–	–	–	–
Inventories	–	–	–	–
Accounts Receivable	2,000	–	2,000	–
Total Cash Outflows	$63,460	$ 0	$12,000	$ 51,460
Current Surplus (Deficit)	$(4,570)	$ 2,195	$ 3,895	$(10,660)
Cash Balance				
Beginning of Period	$16,000	$16,000	$18,195	$ 22,090
Cash Balance				
End of Period	$11,430	$18,195	$22,090	$ 11,430

Observation

There are many times when your assumptions will be wrong and your forecast will suffer as a result. However, if you set your assumptions and monitor them as you go along, you will know when they have fallen short of the mark. As a result, you will be prepared to change your forecast as events unfold.

Once you have made the necessary preparations, you can begin the actual forecasting procedure. As an illustration, refer back to the receipts & disbursements analysis for ABC Publishing. The line items on a short-term cash flow forecast for ABC Publishing would, in all likelihood, be unchanged from the receipts & disbursements analysis. The projection period, however, would extend for an entire year on a monthly basis rather than over the 3 months shown in the analysis.

Multiple Forecasts Are Necessary

Obviously, it would be difficult to develop a format that could make realistic forecasts of the extent and timing of cash flows from, say, 1 month to 5 years in the future. Even if such a forecast did exist, you might not find it all that useful. In a short-term forecast you probably would want to emphasize the details of cash flows into and out of your company. The longer-term forecasts would place the emphasis on the financial aspect of your strategic planning effort. For this reason, your cash-flow information needs will be satisfied best by dividing your forecasting activity into separate areas, one directed at the short-term and one aimed at identifying long-term trends.

Preparing a Short-Term Cash Flow Forecast

Short-term cash flow forecasts are designed to predict your company's cash flow for periods of up to 1 year. In its final form, your forecast will look much like your receipts & disbursements analysis. As with that earlier exercise, the amount of detail you include in the forecasts is up to you and will largely depend on your industry and your own information requirements. Under most conditions, however, a relatively short list of headings will suffice. Cover primarily those items that are subject to management control.

The best way to prepare short-term cash forecasts is on a rolling monthly basis–i.e., the first forecast of the year covers January to December; the next, February to the following January; the next, March through the following February; and so on. In that way, you will receive the earliest possible warning of a cash emergency.

Role of Cash Flow Assumptions

The first step in preparing your forecast is to take a close look at your cash flow performance for the recent past. A review of the past several months can be most helpful in providing information on such items as inventory levels and accounts-receivable performance.

Next, you must make several broad assumptions about your business for the next year. Is it likely to be a good year, a mediocre year or a bad one? Will costs rise at a faster rate than sales or vice versa?

Projecting Line-by-Line

Here, on a line-by-line basis, is how you make your short-term cash flow projections:

Collections

This is by far the most difficult item in the forecast and unquestionably one of the most critical. Keep in mind that your projections for the earliest 1 or 2 months of the forecast are likely to be the most accurate because you have recent sales results and current accounts-receivable information already on hand. After the first month or two, your cash budget and past collection experience will be your primary forecasting tools. Whatever the case, if you bring your forecast up-to-date on a monthly basis, you will always have time to refine your early estimates as time passes.

Cash Sales

Your sales forecast and past experience are your primary guides with this category. Although cash sales are not much easier to predict than collections, they are usually not as large and, therefore, not as critical to the forecast.

Miscellaneous Receipts

Recurring items, such as rents, interest and dividends, are simple matters of fact. Nonrecurring items, such as bank loans, are almost always known to management in advance.

Suppliers

Next to collections, this item will probably require the most investigation. Your sales forecast and inventory policy will be the prime determinants of supplier payments, but production scheduling, purchasing and your accounts-payable policy also will enter into the forecast. Your forecasts for the first few months will be more reliable than those for the future.

Wages and Salaries

This item is usually predictable. The costs of overtime and part-time workers offer the most surprises.

Overhead

Most of the items are payable on a regular basis, so there should be little difficulty in making a forecast for this category if you take price increases into consideration.

Financial Obligations

These include interest, dividends, taxes and debt repayment. Again, recurring items are known to management, and nonrecurring items are matters of management decision.

Special Items

This category is reserved for one-time decisions, such as the sale of an asset. All such matters involve a management decision and are therefore predictable.

Using a Long-Term Cash Flow Forecast

There is a fundamental difference between long-term and short-term forecasts. Short-term forecasts are tactical, concerned with management control of an existing situation. Long-term forecasts are strategic, designed to assist in the development of long-term financing plans that will meet management goals.

Long-term forecasts will indicate not only when you will need additional external financing but also how much extra cash will be required. As a result, forecasting your cash flow needs for the long-term is closely related to strategic planning.

Observation

Always keep in mind that the further out the plan extends, the less reliable the forecast is likely to be.

Just as the receipts & disbursements analysis provided a framework for a short-term cash forecast, the flow-of-funds analysis technique can be adapted to long-term forecasting. You will have to make some changes in format, though, to separate the impact of operational and financial decisions.

Just as it would be foolish to forecast future cash needs in the absence of specific goals, it would be fruitless to plan a future course of action without providing enough cash to get there.

To be useful, long-term forecasts must be updated annually as new budgets are drawn and plans reviewed. Three years appear to be the optimum length for a long-term cash forecast. Financial markets are simply too changeable to permit serious planning for a longer period. However, a shorter cash forecast might not allow you enough time to get ready for a major financing. Obviously, such forecasts, like all predictions, are seldom exact. In general, your long-term cash forecast should mirror your company's planning horizon.

How to Compile Your Long-Term Forecast

Virtually all long-term cash forecasts are based on the adjusted income method. Here, you start with your sales forecast and then adjust the anticipated revenue for various components that are likely to add to or deplete your cash balances.

Determining Your Sources of Cash

There are three basic ways for your company to generate cash. Each must be projected in a different manner:

From Operations

Your operating income projection should be based on your sales forecast. Generally, operating income remains at more or less a fixed percentage of sales. Then add depreciation, a noncash expense, back into operating income. Depreciation estimates can be based on past trends and planned capital expenditures.

From Financing

In this category, cash can come only from asset sales or new financing, both of which involve management decisions. Therefore, the projections you make should be relatively simple.

From Working Capital

This is possibly the thorniest part of your forecast. In this category, you can consider an increase in accounts payable to be a source of cash along with a decline in inventories and/or accounts receivable. Conversely, a decrease in accounts payable represents a use of cash, as does an increase in inventories or accounts receivable.

One method to project accounts receivable is the flow-of-funds calculation. It will tell you how long it takes, on average, to collect each dollar of receivables. For example, if your collection time normally stands at about 27 days, you merely divide forecasted sales by 365 and then multiply by 27 to obtain projected accounts receivable.

You can apply the same principle to accounts payable and inventories by substituting the cost of goods sold for sales. First, divide cost of goods sold for the most recent year by 365 to obtain an average day's cost of goods sold. Then divide that figure into accounts payable and inventories to arrive at days payable outstanding and days inventory outstanding, respectively. Finally, multiply these figures by the average day's cost of goods sold to make your projections.

Projecting Your Uses of Cash

Once you have completed the projections of your sources of funds, you will have calculated many of the uses of funds in the bargain:

For Working Capital

You have already made your working capital projections. Determine a decrease in accounts payable and/or increases in inventories and accounts receivable to indicate how much of your capital these components have absorbed.

For Financial Obligations

Tax payments should be confined to payments actually anticipated. Dividend and interest payments are easily predicted and both debt reduction and capital expenditures involve management discretion to a degree.

> **Caution**
>
> Remember that the first year of a long-term plan must always conform to forecasts made in the short-term plan. Otherwise, managers may find themselves at cross-purposes with one another.

Here are considerations on each of the major categories of information in a long-term forecast:

ABC Publishing Company Long-Term Cash Forecast

Cash Resources:	
Cash From Operations	$113,000
Less: Taxes	47,460
Internal Cash Flow	$ 65,540
Decrease (Increase) in Assets:	
Land & Buildings	–
Plant & Equipment	$(10,000)
Inventories	2,000
Accounts Receivable	(2,000)
Net Asset Change	(10,000)
Net Operating Cash	$ 55,540
Financial Obligations:	
Interest	$ 4,800
Dividends	50,000
Loan Repayment	52,000
Total Obligations	$106,800
Net Cash Requirements	$ 51,260
Planned Financing:	
From Available Cash	$ 1,260
New Credit	10,000
New Borrowing:	
Short-Term	40,000
Long-Term	–
New Equity Capital	–
Total Financing	$ 51,260

Illustration

Refer to the chart to the left. There we have used the information contained in the cash budget for ABC Publishing Company as the basis for a long-term cash forecast. We have also assumed that, as in the flow-of-funds analysis, ABC Publishing decreased inventories by $2,000 and raised accounts receivable by the same amount. In addition, the company purchased a binding machine for $10,000 on credit.

Obviously, this forecast is behind the times. In the real world, the forecast could have been made well before a cash budget was submitted and would extend out for 3 years or more. Nevertheless, it does demonstrate how closely a long-term forecast parallels a flow-of-funds analysis, while at the same time adding information that long-term planners would need to make intelligent decisions.

In ABC's case, no financial surprises are in store. Operating cash makes up more than half the cash needed to meet obligations. The balance of the needed cash is easily met by a short-term loan and new credit.

Long-term cash forecasts normally are updated annually, as strategic plans are reviewed and new budgets drawn. Therefore, even if the plan were a bit wide of the mark, ABC would have time to revise it in subsequent years.

Cash From Operations

This is usually part of your strategic plan. Take into account planned changes in product lines, distribution and so forth.

Taxes

This is a fairly straightforward item, but do not overlook possible tax savings in the future.

Fixed Assets

Payments due for the purchase of new assets (land, buildings, plant and equipment) are usually found in the company's capital budget. Do not forget the costs associated with these assets, such as maintenance and administrative activities.

Noncash Current Assets

These include inventories and accounts receivable. Since inventory and credit policies do not change often, you can usually apply past experience to sales projections for future years to obtain reasonable estimates for changes in inventory and/or accounts receivable.

Financial Obligations

It should be simple to forecast payments due on current obligations (interest, dividends, repayment of loans or bonds), but you may find it difficult to project interest and principal payments on future loans. Dividends are not mandatory, but they should be included here for the sake of clarity.

Net Cash Requirements

If there is to be a cash surplus in your company's future, you will first identify it here. Rather than a net cash requirement, you will come up with a net surplus. You can, of course, make plans to increase your dividends or to invest the surplus for a while.

Available Cash

This reflects drawings from both existing cash balances and cash equivalents (U.S. Treasury bills, certificates of deposit, etc.). A surplus to be invested would be treated as a negative item on this line.

New Credit

Planned purchases, such as the $10,000 binding machine cited in the illustration, are rather easy to identify. However, you may have to look closely to spot a possible need for additional extensions of credit with suppliers.

New Sources of Capital

These final items are strictly based on management decisions. They are the balancing items but also represent the end result of your firm's financial strategy.

Keeping Cash Flow under Control

As you compile your cash forecasts, you are forced to come to grips with possible cash flow problems. This information, plus your analyses of receipts, disbursements and flow-of-funds, will allow you to make any adjustments needed to bring forecasts in line with reality.

Using a Monthly Liquidity Report

A monthly liquidity report is the final informational tool in the cash flow management system. Easily prepared from monthly statements and previous forecasts, it will give you the information you need to make day-to-day working decisions concerning your cash flow.

The report not only tells you how far off your cash flow forecasts might be but also sums up the state of your resources, thus giving you the information needed to make quick decisions.

The Right Cash Flow Yardsticks

Preparing a liquidity report is more a matter of organizing existing information than gathering new data. All the information needed for the report should be readily available shortly after the end of each month. (See page 24 for how your liquidity report might look.)

Observation

The definition of net cash provided by operations is the key to the statement. Normally, this figure encompasses cash raised from sales, less out-of-pocket cost of goods sold and other out-of-pocket expenses:

- Cash sales means just that. Notes and accounts receivable do not qualify and must be deducted from sales. However, if notes or accounts receivable decline, extra cash is coming in, so sales should be adjusted upward.
- Cash cost of goods sold consists of the actual dollars spent for manufacturing during the period. An increase in inventory means that extra cash was spent, so the cost of goods sold should be adjusted upward. A downturn in inventories lowers your cost of goods sold. Conversely, a decrease in accounts or notes payable indicates additional cash payments and raises the cost of goods sold, while an increase lowers the item.

Liquidity Report ABC Corporation–Cash Flow Statement	
Net Cash Provided by Operations	$37,000
Uses of Cash:	
Dividends	(20,000)
Interest (Net of Tax)	(5,000)
Financing Activities	7,000
Increase (Decrease) in Net Cash	$19,000
Net Cash Balance–Beginning of Year	$15,000
Net Cash Balance–End of Year	$34,000

Because it can be difficult to derive cash flow information from the usual financial statements, many managers gauge their cash flow either by adding depreciation back into net income or by using working capital from operations as a substitute. However, both measures are often at odds with actual cash flow performance and can give off confusing or even misleading signals:

Net Income Plus Depreciation

Even though many financial people do use this formula (cash flow = net income + depreciation) to define cash flow, it is not entirely accurate. The formula represents more a measurement of profitability, or what some business researchers call gross cash flow, than net cash flow. For example, it is a paradox of business that companies with little or no growth usually have fewer cash problems than high-profit, rapid-growth firms.

Working Capital from Operations

Again, some use the working-capital formula to measure cash flow.

(current assets – current liabilities = working capital)

Even though working capital is expressed in dollars, it cannot be spent like cash. Working capital is a concept that does not pay day-to-day bills; only cash does.

Calculating Your Real Cash Flow

A cash-basis presentation in your flow-of-funds statement avoids the potential problems of relying too heavily on working capital trends while, at the same time, it quickly gives you a clear picture of your company's overall liquidity. The flow-of-funds or cash flow statement can be structured a number of ways to reflect changes in your cash position. None of them is unduly complicated.

To be useful, your flow-of-funds statement should tell you whether your operations are generating enough cash to support your expenditures. Specifically, you will want to know how much cash was generated from operations, how much cash was used and whether your net cash position improved or deteriorated during the year. In condensed form, your statement might read like this:

> In this case, the net cash generated by ABC Corporation's overall operations was more than sufficient to take care of interest charges and a hefty dividend payment. Moreover, a financing provided a further increment to cash resources. All in all, cash and cash equivalents more than doubled during the year.

Keep in mind that other expenses must also be adjusted to reflect cash transactions. If accrued liabilities declined, cash was used to pay them off, so add that amount to cash expenses. An increase in accrued liabilities should be deducted from cash expenses. If prepaid expenses rise, add the amount to cash expenses; if they decline, reduce cash expenses commensurately.

Making Your Cash Count

Be aware of the opportunities that can increase the cash you have on hand to meet short-term expenses. For example:

- Participation in electronic funds transfer (EFT) programs generally leads to a reduction in payment costs, compared to the use of checks. Moreover, by arranging for discounts in return for fast payment, receivables carrying costs can be reduced.
- Consider keeping your money in a money market account. By combining your present checking account with a money market deposit account, you can put your liquid assets to work and save yourself most activity fees in the bargain. (See on page 34 for more ideas.) Look for other methods or programs that banks have to improve cash management.

Managing a Financial Emergency

Even if you make all the right moves in managing your cash flow, including reliable forecasts, accurate analysis reports and up-to-date liquidity studies, you may still wind up in the midst of a cash crunch. The reason is simple: Many financial emergencies are caused by events outside management's control, such as an international financial crisis or a severe recession.

Some of the early warning signs of a cash emergency include:

- A series of relatively short-term cash problems.
- A prolonged drop in sales that has not been met with appropriate belt-tightening.
- Rising expenditures that have failed to generate proportionately higher sales volume.
- A need for short-term loans to cover normal operating expenses.

When these signs start flashing, a company can consider itself in a cash crisis and should take decisive action in the following areas:

Dig Up Untapped Cash Reserves

Here are some suggested moves:

- Obtain the necessary information to monitor the emergency. Monthly data on receivables and past-due accounts are not timely enough; have accounting prepare these reports weekly.
- Another essential tool is the cash forecast. Each week, gather data showing cash on hand and in the bank, short-term investments, accounts receivable, inventories, any unused lines of credit and accounts payable. For each of these categories, the report should forecast expected balances for 30–90 days ahead and compare actual balances with projected balances. This type of report not only helps in making decisions but also is vital in convincing a bank to renegotiate your loan or extend additional credit, if necessary. (See chart below.)

Balance– End of Month	Current Forecast	Month Actual	Percentage Change	Forecast Coming Month
Cash on Hand and in Bank	_____	_____	_____	_________
Cash Equivalents (Short-Term Investments)	_____	_____	_____	_________
Accounts Receivable	_____	_____	_____	_________
Accounts Payable	_____	_____	_____	_________
Inventories	_____	_____	_____	_________
Unused Lines of Credit	_____	_____	_____	_________

- Reform your collection procedures. Bill customers upon receipt of the order or on the day of shipment. Set up a cash-concentration system, such as a network of lockboxes (see page 31) to hasten the deposit of payments to your accounts. Also, make it a practice to call or write to all clients/customers promptly once their accounts become overdue and start imposing late fees on bills that are more than 30 days overdue.
- Get tough on credit. Put all but your best customers on a cash-only or 50 percent down-payment basis.
- Sell your receivables to a factoring service (see page 45).
- Liquidate all assets that are not needed within a reasonable time: materials or supplies that will not be used within a year; computers and other equipment that are used less than half of the typical workweek; idle real estate; and obsolete inventory. (See page 47 for more information.)
- Consider restructuring the company pension plan to free excess cash. Many plans are over funded and smaller contributions may be possible. Or you may want to cut back on the pension benefits your firm offers. If so, you need to check with a pension expert (not necessarily the company's regular lawyer or accountant) and consider the impact on employee morale.

Slow Down Cash Outflow

Here are some ways to do it:

- Wherever possible, negotiate with vendors and lenders to postpone payments. Point out that creditors have a better chance of getting paid if they agree to stretch terms an additional 30 days.
- Use cash flow analysis (see pages 14-17) to pay checks on the last possible date for earning discounts. This will increase your company's interest income.

Cut Costs

Obvious moves such as layoffs and capital spending cutbacks can hamper the company's ability to recover after the cash crisis. Consider these moves first:

- Call an immediate halt to all cash-draining functions and operations, including marginally profitable products or services.

- Analyze profitability of salespeople, accounts and territories. Tell sales managers to boost performance of marginal performers or terminate them. Hire manufacturers' representatives to cover relatively thin territories. Put marginal accounts on a cash-only basis.
- Consider restructuring sales bonuses and incentives to reflect contributions to profits, as well as sales volume.
- Put employees on semi-monthly paychecks to reduce payroll processing costs.

Once the crisis is over, do not forget the tools that helped you through the emergency. For example, the cash forecast should be continued, but on a monthly instead of a weekly basis. The forecast is vital in predicting future crises in plenty of time so that inventories, payroll, marketing programs, borrowing and credit policies can be adjusted accordingly.

Recommendation

The American Management Association, at *www.amanet.org* conducts seminars on cash management in a number of cities. The Treasury Management Association also offers educational training; contact them at *www.tmany.org* (this one is for New York, but there are many similar regional offices).

Ways to Fend off a Cash Crunch

All financial emergencies have one common characteristic: If not dealt with quickly, they create more problems and become a drag on every facet of operations and planning. For this reason, a financial contingency plan should be part and parcel of every cash-management program. The objective: to quicken your response time to unforeseen financial strains.

No two financial contingency plans will be the same simply because no two companies are the same. Nevertheless, every plan should contain the following three basic elements:

1. An Early Warning System

We have observed in previous pages that early warning is the key to effective cash management. Nowhere is this truer than in dealing with a cash crisis.

The first step is to determine which key variables have the greatest impact on the financial viability of your firm. These variables will differ from firm to firm. For some, inventories will be the culprit. Others might find loan interest to be the chief burden.

Next, keep a close watch on the assumptions that have been built into your cash flow forecasts. Very often, the fact that one or more of those assumptions has proven to be invalid is the earliest warning sign you will have of impending difficulty. For instance, if your forecast assumes that interest rates will drift lower and they go up instead, your company could be headed for trouble. This is particularly true if you will need to do some financing.

Finally, you should take a close look at your company's history to find the cause and cure of past financial crises. History may not repeat itself; but if it does, your knowledge of how past difficulties have been overcome should yield positive results when dealing with the next crisis.

Observation

Each type of action has its own strengths and drawbacks. For instance, timing changes are easy to implement but can go only so far and only serve to delay the inevitable in a protracted crisis. Volume changes can change cash flow patterns in a hurry but are effective only when the emergency is related to declining sales. Policy actions, including irreversible ones like selling a division, offer the most fertile field for cutting expenses. However, they can take time and can delay a recovery. All things considered, the best approach usually involves a combination of decisions, each supplementing and complementing the other.

2. Your Priorities

Once you have identified an emerging financial crisis, you will need to know three things: (1) what can be done; (2) how long it will take; and (3) how much cash you can raise. The best way to obtain this information is to establish a list of priorities organized around the four types of management decisions discussed in the beginning of this section.

- Timing changes;
- policy changes;
- volume changes; and
- irreversible policy changes.

To that you could add potential financing sources, so your priority list probably would wind up looking something like the sample on the next page.

Priority List		
Type of Action	Estimated Cash	Response Time
Timing Changes		
Speed Collections	________	________
Delay Supplier Payments	________	________
Delay Capital Expenditure	________	________
Other	________	________
Policy Changes		
Reduce Inventory	________	________
Reduce Dividend	________	________
Cut Capital Expenditure	________	________
Reduce Expenses:		
Administration	________	________
Production	________	________
Sales	________	________
Volume Changes		
Cut Part-Time	________	________
Cut Overtime	________	________
Cut Shift	________	________
Layoffs	________	________
Irreversible Policy Changes		
Liquidate Assets	________	________
Financing:		
Short-Term	________	________
Long-Term	________	________
Equity	________	________

3. An Emergency Reserve

Once you understand what kind of actions can be taken in an emergency and how long they might take, you can set up a sort of insurance policy in the form of an emergency reserve. The size of the reserve is up to you. It should depend on the length of time that it will take to mobilize your other cash resources and the estimated size of a cash drain during an emergency. For example, if you estimate that it would take 4 business days for an initial emergency response to yield cash and your maximum cash drain could be as high as $5,000 per day in an emergency, you would need an emergency reserve of $20,000 for full protection.

Such reserves are usually held in money market funds or in an interest-bearing account. However, an unused line of credit would suffice if the funds were committed by the bank.

Caution

To be effective, the reserve must always be available at a moment's notice. Therefore, most traditional investments, such as Treasury bills, are out even though they may be perfectly safe.

Managing Growing Pains

During periods of revenue growth, chief executives tend to focus on maintaining that growth and introducing new products or services. While your attention is elsewhere, watch out for increased bad debts, longer collection periods and employee theft. Here is how:

Staff Up

Credit checking is labor-intensive. If your credit department does not grow with sales, some credit checks will be superficial, increasing your sales to companies that will take 60 or 90 days to pay or will not pay at all.

Review Your Down-Payment Policy

To shorten the collection period for new accounts and combat bad debts, you can raise your minimum down payment from, say, 10 percent to 20 percent of the sale.

Try a Lockbox System

This is an arrangement with your bank that is designed to speed the receipt and processing of customers' checks. Your customer base is divided into territories. The customers mail payments to a post office box within their territory, so as to reduce the amount of time checks spend in the mail. The checks are picked up from the boxes by the nearest branch or affiliate of your bank, at which point they are recorded and sent to the customer's nearby bank for cashing. Once the checks clear, the funds can be credited to your account by electronic funds transfer. Your bank collects a fee for administering the lockbox system.

> **Observation**
> When revenues grow quickly, small companies sometimes outgrow their treasurers. In this case, it is often better to hire an experienced full-time person than to have an inexperienced treasurer try to follow up on a consultant's recommendations.

Lockboxes are practical if your customer base is spread over a wide geographic area. They are common with larger companies. If your size or sales pattern does not justify lockboxes, have your salespeople send checks from all customers directly to your bank for deposit.

Anticipate Fronting

In fronting, salespeople claim credit sales to nonexistent companies. They put up the down payment from their own pockets and then reimburse themselves from the commission. To protect your company from this practice, which can occur when credit department work is spotty, pay only a percentage of your standard commission on a credit sale and hold the remainder until you have received full payment.

Keep a Close Watch on Your Bookkeeper

A bookkeeper whose work is not audited regularly may work too slowly, delaying the deposit of customer checks. The later those checks are deposited, the more the funds benefit your customers rather than your company.

Summary

The cash management system set forth in this section can make a considerable contribution to your firm. Thoughtfully used, it will identify cash flow imbalances before they become major problems and point the way toward solutions. Consequently, with your cash flow on an even keel, you can devote much more time and attention to areas where they most properly belong–building your company's revenues in a scope and sequence that contribute to an overall profitable operation.

2 Cash Management Strategies

It is important to keep a sharp eye on your cash flow pattern. A widening of the gap between the time that product costs are incurred and revenues associated with those costs are posted will eventually lead to a chronic cash deficiency. A narrowing will erode your company's margins because you will be accumulating assets that are making no contribution whatsoever to your firm.

The gap between your cash outflow and income is often influenced by external forces, such as interest rates, business conditions and the inflation rate. So you will want to pay special attention to it when the economy is in transition.

Measuring Your Cash Flow Time Lag

The easiest way to keep tabs on the time lag between your cash outflow and income is by using the working capital to sales ratio (working capital ÷ sales) as a yardstick. The cash part of your working capital pool can be viewed as the funds needed to replace the dollars used in production until new sales dollars actually come in.

Unless your operations change radically, your firm will usually require a certain amount of working capital to back up each sales dollar, whether sales move up or down. For example, if your working capital to sales ratio stands at .25 with, say, $2 million in sales this year backed by $500,000 of working capital, it should remain near that level next year, whether sales rise by $2 million or decrease to $1.8 million.

Any marked decline in the ratio would mean that the relative size of your working capital pool has been depleted due to a stretching out of the time lag between cash outflow and inflow. Conversely, a rise in the ratio would imply a shortening of the time lag, an unnecessary rise of your working capital and consequent pressure on your profit margins.

Look Behind the Ratio

Once you spot a significant change in your working capital to sales ratio, you should investigate further to isolate the reason for the change. Generally, you should center your investigation on the two most important noncash components of your current assets:

- **Inventories**
  An unexpected drop in inventories can, of course, endanger your production schedule, just as a bulge can eat up your cash. Here, the trend of your inventory turnover ratio (cost of goods sold ÷ inventory) will give you valuable clues on your appropriate inventory levels. If this ratio is unusually low, your inventories are probably too high. Conversely, an abnormally high ratio indicates depleted inventories.
- **Accounts Receivable**
  A sudden buildup in receivables without an accompanying sales gain can squeeze profitability, just as a drop in receivables without an accompanying increase in cash assets can foreshadow financial difficulties. Here, your average collection period (see page 75) can be used to measure the effectiveness of your current credit policy. Another valid measure might be your receivables turnover ratio (sales ÷ accounts receivable). The higher that ratio, the better.

Improve Liquidity with a Money Market Account

If your company normally keeps even a moderate liquid balance in your checking or depository account, your account is costing you hundreds or even thousands of dollars each year in lost interest. Couple this with the 5-cent to 15-cent per item bank activity fee for check deposits and the total cost of maintaining your primary business account in its present form can be considerable.

For instance, keeping even a modest average of $10,000 in your checking account would cost $450 or more in lost interest over a year's time. Depositing only 50 checks per month would cost another $60 per year, assuming an activity fee of 10 cents per check.

However, by combining your present checking account with a money market deposit account, you can put your liquid assets to work and save yourself most of the activity fees in the bargain.

The key to the operation is the way that bank money market accounts are structured. Under present rules, you are restricted to three check withdrawals per month, but most banks allow up to 10 ATM withdrawals monthly and an unlimited amount of deposits without a fee.

Thus, by using a bank money market account as your primary deposit account, you can avoid deposit fees. Then, every 10 days, you transfer as much as is needed to your checking account. In the meantime, your funds are earning a satisfactory rate of interest.

Observation

You do not necessarily need to seek out a corporate money market account. While terms will vary from bank to bank, corporate money market accounts usually offer somewhat lower interest rates than those intended primarily for individuals and may impose some fees.

What to Look for

In seeking out the right bank money market account to use as your depository–or repository for excess–look for these characteristics:

- **No deposit service charges**
  As we have stressed, this is one of the prime considerations in choosing a bank money market fund.
- **Daily compounding**
  Most banks compound interest daily on money market accounts just to compete with money market funds. But make sure that your bank is not one of the exceptions.
- **Low minimum balance**
  You never know when an unexpected development might require the temporary use of your liquid assets.

- **Full interest accrual**
  Day of deposit/day of withdrawal is best. Be certain that your bank does not wait until the end of the month to begin crediting interest on the deposits.

Money market funds and bank money market accounts may be safe investments, but the yields are fairly low these days. Recently, for example, most money market funds were paying in the 1.50 percent to 4 percent range, and bank money market accounts were in the 2.5 to 2.75 percent range. If your company keeps a modest amount in the bank, such as an average balance of $10,000, an extra 0.5 per year is only $50 (pretax). To receive a real excess of cash, your company would have to keep a much larger balance.

When Your Aim Is to Park Excess Cash

Here, you should evaluate several factors in addition to yield. To find the money market account with the highest net return, poll different banks for their monthly charges for maintenance and withdrawals, as well as penalties for exceeding an account's monthly check limit. Then look for an account with:

- **Appropriate minimum balances**
  Banks pay higher rates on accounts with larger minimums. In that case, you must be sure your company will maintain the minimum for a high-yielding account. Otherwise, you may end up forfeiting all interest on your funds when your balance drops below the account minimum.

- **Advantageous tiering**
  Look for an account that raises its rate as your balance rises. On the other hand, avoid tiering that penalizes your account when balances drop. Accounts such as these may pay only passbook rates when balances drop below $15,000.

- **Suitable balance caps**
  In some cases, banks will not pay interest on balances that exceed $100,000. This can force you to open more than one money market account and thus complicate your cash management program.

Observation

A corporate money market account is appropriate if you or your treasurer wears several hats and lacks the time to move cash in and out of riskier and higher-yielding financial instruments. Also, there is no reason why you cannot make your initial deposit in a bank outside your community if it offers a better return.

- **Daily interest compounding**
  Avoid banks that calculate simple interest on a monthly basis.

Mailing Policies Can Improve Cash Management

There is no free lunch when your bank tries to sell cash management services to your company. As a result, it is sensible to examine your company's existing collection and disbursement practices before paying your bank for any new cash management services. Several commonly overlooked procedures might improve your company's handling of incoming customer payments and disbursements to creditors. For example:

Speed incoming payments via the following procedures:

- **Mail invoices according to the dispatch priorities of the Post Office.**
  Your local post office dispatches first-class and overnight mail to overnight delivery areas before dispatching first-class mail to so-called third-day areas. To take advantage, have your mail room process invoices to distant customers first. This will speed delivery of these invoices without delaying the delivery of bills to overnight areas.
- **Coordinate invoice mailing with dispatch times at your Post Office.**
  If your post office mails at noon, 2 p.m. and 5 p.m., get invoices to your post office by noon to guarantee that those invoices will not wait a day at the post office while it processes local mail.
- **Do not use business reply envelopes for incoming customer payments.**
  The post office tends to accumulate such envelopes, delivering them in bunches. This can add a day or more to your collection period, and you pay the postage.
- **Use so-called courtesy reply envelopes for incoming payments.**
  The post office does not mass these envelopes for delivery. Meanwhile, you can speed the delivery of these bills to the appropriate employee in-house by adding bar codes, identification marks or color coding to the envelopes.
- **Direct customer payments to a post office box.**
  Your employees should pick up from this post office box several times daily. This will eliminate the extra time required for regular delivery by a mail carrier.

Slow disbursements while maintaining your credit rating in these ways:

- **Use express mail for large, just-in-time payments.**
  This allows your company to retain its funds for as long as possible without paying late or missing a trade discount.
- **Use your own envelopes when paying bills.**
  In many cases, this tactic causes your check to wander for an extra day through your creditor's collection system.
- **Mail payments so that they arrive on Friday.**
  Here, your company retains credit for the funds in its bank account for the weekend.

Use Availability Schedules on Check Clearance

An availability schedule can be a valuable tool for minimizing the collection time on checks deposited to your company's account. In banking parlance, availability is the time it takes for your bank to make available the funds from customers' checks deposited to your account. It is the time that elapses in the clearing process.

The sooner the funds are made available to you, the more efficient your cash management program will be. Even if you reduce your clearing process by only 1 day, you should be able to earn considerably more interest for your company over a year's time. Take these steps:

Determine How Your Bank Assigns Availability

Not all banks use the same methods to determine availability. Some use a blanket policy and assign a certain number of days to all checks. This may be an arbitrary figure, or it may be related to the average number of days it takes the bank to collect funds. Others take a different approach by assigning availability on a check-by-check basis.

Your bank's basic policy toward determining availability is the most important factor in making your funds available in the shortest possible time. However, a number of other factors can also make a difference. Here are some questions to ask:

- **Does your bank clear through the Federal Reserve System?**
  If so, the Fed will not delay availability to your bank for more than 2 days, regardless of how long the actual collection process takes.

- **Does your state impose check clearance deadlines?**
  If so, you have the advantage of knowing the very longest your bank can legally take.
- **Does your bank use a round-the-clock processing system?**
  Many banks use 24-hour computerized check processing and a widespread check transportation system to speed up availability. Such systems often cut availability time in half.
- **Does your bank set deadlines?**
  Many banks set deadlines for deposits, after which availability is delayed by 1 day. The deadline may be at 11:30 a.m. or even 9:30 a.m.
  Often, strict adherence to bank deposit rules is the easiest way to speed up availability.

Gather Information for Your Availability Schedule

Once you are familiar with state laws and the clearing practices of the various banks in your area, you will need to know three things to determine which bank best fits your needs:

1. You must have a firm idea of where your checks are drawn.
2. You should know when the bulk of your checks are received.
3. You should be aware of how long it takes to process the checks before deposit.

Your present bank will usually help you determine where your checks come from. Your accounts receivable department can give you a firm handle on the other two points.

Draw Up the Schedule

Once you have this information in hand, you can compare your needs with the parameters set down by various banks in your area. Take the availability schedules assigned to categories of checks by the banks you are considering. Then review your collections to see how many of your checks fall into each category to estimate how soon the funds would be available to you at each of the banks.

You may find it useful to compile two schedules, one segregating the physical number of checks and the other using dollar amounts as a guide. In this regard, banks in your area should offer some assistance.

Act on Your Findings

If your primary bank is comparatively slow in clearing checks, a move to the competition might improve your cash flow. Weigh all the factors, however. Advantageous lines of credit and a good relationship with your banker, for example, are important factors. Also, have a talk with your current banker. Perhaps adjustments can be made. Most banks today strive to be competitive.

Zero-Balance Account Can Provide Liquidity

Once used chiefly by large corporations, zero-balance accounts are now available to small companies as cash management tools. Zero-balance accounts (ZBAs), or wash accounts as some banks refer to them, allow you to take full advantage of bank float and collection time without subjecting your company to the possible penalties or embarrassment involved in returned checks.

Simply put, a ZBA is an agreement with your bank allowing you to write checks against an account that contains no funds. As the checks clear, the bank notes the amounts of the debits and informs you, usually by telephone, of the amount of the overdraft. Near the close of the business day, you authorize a transfer from a master account to cover the total debit and return the account to a zero balance. That way, you keep the full use of your funds until the checks drawn on the account actually clear. The bank is compensated because the funds to cover the outstanding checks remain on deposit with it, even if they are temporarily parked in the master account.

Payroll accounts are by far the most common way for corporations to use ZBAs simply because they are regular and predictable.

However, you can use ZBAs to cover other disbursements. Supplier payments can be made through ZBAs, particularly if

Illustration

You use a ZBA to meet your $100,000 weekly payroll. Each Thursday, your supervisors hand out the payroll checks, but no transfers to your ZBA payroll account are needed yet. A few transfers are made on Friday, but the bulk of the funds are not released until Monday or Tuesday. Thus, you retain the use of the funds over the weekend, possibly placing them in interest-bearing money market instruments such as banker's acceptances or commercial paper. The rewards of this technique can be significant. For example, if you gained an average of 3 extra days' interest on your $100,000 weekly payroll, you could earn more than $1,000 annually at current rates.

sent to distant locations. Installment payments for machinery or equipment might be another candidate, as would lease payments. Keep in mind, however, that payments made to a bank normally would not be considered for a ZBA account because they would clear too quickly to be of much value.

Since ZBA accounts have become a more or less common cash management practice, fees have come down considerably. However, they still vary a great deal, depending on your region and your company's relationship with its bank. At one bank, for example, an inactive ZBA might be charged only $12 per month while an active user might pay in the thousands.

Take Advantage of a Prime Tax Break

If your company invests in another U.S. company, any stock dividends you receive generally qualify for a 70 percent to 80 percent tax exclusion. Example: Your corporation buys $10,000 worth of ABC Co. stock, which pays a $600 (6 percent) annual dividend. If between 70 percent and 80 percent (we take 75 percent as the average) is excluded from tax, only $150 will be taxable. Assuming a 34 percent corporate tax bracket, you would owe only $51 in taxes and keep $549, for a 5.49 percent after-tax return.

Today, even higher after-tax returns may be possible, but it is hard to know which stock dividends are safer than others. Therefore, you may want to invest through a mutual fund. There is a handful of such funds on the market now, offered by fund families such as Colonial, Pilgrim and Putnam. You can usually distinguish them by the words corporate cash in their names.

Not all corporate cash funds are alike. Among the main investment categories: high-yielding common stocks, such as utilities; adjustable-rate preferreds (ARPs), short-term paper that is rolled over periodically; and high-yield preferreds, the stock equivalent of junk bonds.

Depending on how the funds invest, yields may vary greatly. Fidelity's Select Utility fund paid a yield of a whopping 46.9 percent in a 12-month period. That was a standout, however, in a group where the yield over the same period could be as low as 3.1 percent. Of course, in choosing funds that reach for high yields, you are likely to assume a much greater risk to get the higher payout.

Other factors to consider:

- **Look behind the yield**
  In theory, corporate cash funds will be stable vehicles. If interest rates rise, for example, ARPs will pay higher yields while utility stocks and high-yield preferreds will lose value. And vice versa. But these vehicles are relatively new, so be sure that you know what is in a fund and that you are comfortable with management's philosophy before you invest.
- **Watch for ease of transfer**
  You should make sure you can transfer money in and out of a corporate cash fund quickly when you need to move your money around. Ask about wire transfer privileges before you invest in a fund. Look for same-day crediting of deposits and free check writing, too.

Get Premium Rates with Offbeat Investments

Currently, the more commonly used short-term investment vehicles, such as 30-day negotiable CDs and 90-day Treasury bills, are yielding about 4.6 percent. Small firms, however, can obtain somewhat better-than-average returns by concentrating on the following, less commonly known money market instruments:

Repos

These are repurchase agreements in which the investors lend money in exchange for securities for a period of time, ranging from overnight to 3 days. When the period expires, investors surrender the securities in exchange for their principal, plus interest at a rate that usually exceeds the federal funds rate by as much as 10 to 15 basis points. (A basis point equals one hundredth of a percent.)

If you are interested in repos, work through a bank that you have chosen carefully. First, you will want a bank that pools repos, since the agreements themselves are usually for amounts over $1 million. Some banks arrange for repo pools; some do not. Also, make sure the bank sets high standards for repo transactions. It should, for instance, only use dealers regulated by the Security and Exchange Commission (SEC). In this way, you can avoid the riskier areas of the repo market.

Cash Management Bills

These are issued by the U.S. Treasury and can be an attractive alternative to T-bills. Cash management bills are issued on an irregular basis to cover specific cash shortfalls in the Treasury Department and are rarely refinanced. If the specific maturity date fits your investment needs, you will find that cash management bills carry rates about 10 basis points over those of T-bills.

Companies can purchase cash management bills through a local bank or broker. Denominations start at $1 million, so find a bank that pools them. Local banks and brokers do charge for paperwork. Banks' fees are generally lower than those of brokers.

Ineligible Banker's Acceptances

A banker's acceptance is essentially a sales contract that is backed up by a bank. They are used mainly to facilitate international trade. With the combined credit of the corporation and the bank behind them, banker's acceptances are popular money market instruments, changing hands nearly as freely as Treasury bills.

Mainstream banker's acceptances are eligible. They cover readily marketable commodities and have a specific maturity date. Therefore, they can be redeemed at most banks, providing ready liquidity. They might yield 20 basis points over T-bills. Ineligible banker's acceptances are oddballs. They are no less creditworthy, but they cover specialty goods or they have estimated (not fixed) maturity dates. Thus, they are not as liquid, and they yield as much as 25 basis points more than eligible banker's acceptances.

Banker's acceptances come in different dollar amounts. To locate attractive ones, let your bank know that you are interested in such vehicles and spell out your size and maturity preferences.

Letters of Credit: Alternative to Cash Advances

Executives who are trying to retain cash in their companies often overlook letters of credit (L/C) as a cash management tool. As a result, their companies make cash advances on certain contracts even though letters of credit would be an acceptable alternative to their suppliers. For companies that are expanding rapidly or that borrow at several points over prime, this can be expensive.

When They Are the Right Tool

Banks follow different procedures when honoring different letters of credit. But the effect is the same for all: A buyer retains the use of his money until payment; a supplier is guaranteed payment by the buyer's bank.

Illustration

A dye company wants a chemical manufacturer to produce 300 drums of specialty dye. The dye will take 60 days to produce. Once prepared, the dye will be of no use to any other firm. The buyer's alternatives: Pay upfront or convince the chemical company to accept a letter of credit. In this and similar situations, a L/C is the appropriate financing and cash management tool.

If your company chooses to use a letter of credit, it may:

- **Reduce your costs**
  You will have to pay various fees for a letter of credit, depending on your relationship with the issuing bank and the complexity of the transaction. There are issuing fees, confirmation fees, advisory fees and others. Still, when you figure the borrowing costs you are probably better off using a L/C rather than borrowing to finance an upfront down payment.
- **Let you keep your flexibility**
  If you have a solid relationship with your bank, you can get a L/C without having to pledge collateral, such as cash or marketable securities. However, if your bank demands collateral, your corporate liquidity will be reduced, so a L/C would not be such an attractive option.

To use a L/C, you must do the following:

- **Trust the supplier**
  Letters of credit are either documentary or standby. With documentary letters of credit, the banker pays the supplier when documents show it has shipped the goods. With standby letters of credit, the bank pays–no questions asked–when the supplier says the buyer has violated the contract. Problem: If the supplier is dishonest, your bank may pay on the L/C even if no performance has occurred, then come after your company for reimbursement.
- **Know a willing bank**
  To use letters of credit, your company must have a steady relationship with a larger bank. The bank's evaluation of your company's creditworthiness and the overall account importance affect both

availability and pricing. As a senior vice president at a New Jersey bank warned, "With a standby letter of credit, we put our customer through the same drill as [for] lending money."

> **Observation**
>
> A buyer retains his cash when substituting a letter of credit for a large cash advance. Meanwhile, a supplier facilitates an otherwise difficult sale while being guaranteed payment. For this reason, suppliers often ask marginal accounts or companies with short credit histories to get a letter of credit before going ahead with a deal.

- **Know how to review the documents**
  Auditors have found banks that have issued up to half their letters of credit with mistakes. As a result, a buyer needs a staff member who can review key areas in the documentation. These include a specific description of the conditions that trigger payment; a clear designation of those persons who can receive payment; and an arbitration clause requiring that disputes be settled in the spirit, not the letter, of the contract.

A Commercial Factor May Help

If your company needs financing to build up inventories in advance of heavy shipping dates or has trouble handling swollen accounts receivable after a peak season, a factor might be able to put your business on a more even keel. In a factoring arrangement, your company actually sells its receivables to the factor, which then assumes all credit risks without recourse.

Factoring has long been a common business practice in the textile and apparel industries, but it has been slow to spread to other industries. This is because factors have historically adopted an insular attitude and because customers in industries not accustomed to factoring are sometimes uncomfortable with having their accounts assigned to third parties.

Along with a change in attitude has come a variety of new factoring forms and services that can be tailored to suit a wide range of needs:

- **Maturity factoring**
  In the traditional form of factoring, you sell the accounts receivable to the factor and receive your money when the invoice matures (usually in 30 days). The customer is notified and instructed to forward payment directly to the factor, which handles all collection and bookkeeping chores.

- **Non-notification factoring**
  In this type of arrangement, your company handles the bookkeeping and collects payments. You get a break on the fees, and your customer does not have to know about the factoring arrangement.
- **Advance payments**
  Factoring has a big advantage over accounts receivable loans in that you receive the full amount of your receivables as they come due, less a factoring fee of 1 percent to 2 percent. With a bank loan, you receive only 70 percent to 80 percent of the receivables' face value. Also, factors offer cash advances on receivables not yet due. Usually rates charged on advances vary between 1 percent and 3 percent over prime. Some factors even offer over-advances, which are essentially unsecured or secured loans to cover peak inventory buildups in anticipation of a bulge in receivables.

Can you use a factor? If you believe that the time, talent and resources now being directed to credit operations might be better spent on sales or production, you can probably use the services of a factor. This is particularly true if you periodically need additional cash to ease seasonal or cyclical financial obligations.

Keep in mind that factoring fees typically run between 1 percent and 2 percent of the amount factored. However, by using a factor, you may be able to reduce or even eliminate your credit department.

Observation

Your biggest decision on whether or not to use the services of a factor will come in the area of credit extensions. The factor will set the rules on credit availability. Since the factor wants to keep losses down, that person's rules are likely to be much tougher than your own.

Consider Selling Unneeded Materials

Although cost-minded companies have probably reduced inventories and other purchases to minimum levels already, many have failed to take the next logical step: converting into cash any liquid assets that are not needed within a reasonable time frame.

The same considerations apply for capital investments such as equipment, except that depreciation has to be factored in. Consult an accountant, banker or financial adviser on the costs/benefits of selling versus holding onto equipment that may eventually be used.

Do You Have Unneeded Assets?

There can be considerable unneeded assets in almost any company–perhaps more than anyone cares to admit. They often represent mistakes in investment decisions, or they may be the result of changes in company direction. Unneeded assets may include items such as a computer that probably would not be fully used for several years, idle real estate, obsolete inventory and surplus paper, parts or other supplies.

Illustration

Consider the reselling of $5,000 worth of materials that, due to a drop in demand, would not be needed for 3 years. Sell them for, say, $4,000 and the company gets immediate use of that cash. In addition, the company gets a tax savings (at a 34 percent tax rate) of $340 from writing off the $1,000 loss on the sale. If the price of the materials is expected to remain fairly stable, it is likely that the company would get a greater return by investing that $4,340 than it would by holding onto the material for 3 years, especially when carrying costs are figured in.

To uncover assets that can be converted to cash, consider the following courses of action:

- **Identify disposable inventories, equipment, furnishings and supplies.**
  Specify that any property not having a foreseeable use in 1 or 2 years be designated as surplus.
- **Establish procedures for disposal.**
  Usually the purchasing manager is in the best position to determine which property is true surplus and how best to dispose of it. Legal authority from the owner or board will have to be given to this individual to sell to outsiders. In many cases, equipment or material may be transferable to other operations, realizing immediate savings. Much of the remainder can be sold to employees, dealers or even to scrap yards, or perhaps to a reputable liquidation or auction firm.
- **Track the costs and benefits.**
  The cost of administering the program should be measured against the income produced by liquidating the equipment or supplies versus their original acquisition costs or book value.

Observation

Many companies cashing in unused assets have recouped 50 cents to 70 cents per dollar of original investment. Yet a firm may not have the value of such property until managers identify disposable assets.

Fine-Tune Accounts Payable

Most companies routinely monitor accounts receivable but keep a rather loose rein on accounts payable. To conserve your financial resources, however, you should stretch out your payments as long as possible without short-changing or angering suppliers.

Calculating Days Purchases Outstanding

This ratio compares current accounts payable with annual purchases, as follows:

Current accounts payable ÷ total annual purchases x 365

Basically, this ratio will tell you the average time you take to pay your suppliers. For example, if your annual purchases amount to $703,000 and your current accounts payable account stands at $94,000, your calculation would look like this:

$94,000 ÷ $703,000 x 365 = 48.8 days

Since it takes your company an average of 49 days to pay your suppliers, your production cycle theoretically should be somewhat shorter. If you can produce and sell your product in less than 49 days, your inventory needs are, in effect, being financed entirely by your suppliers. To the extent that your production cycle exceeds the 49-day mark, you are picking up your own inventory tab.

Calculating Accounts Payable Velocity

While days purchases outstanding can give you important information on the effectiveness of your payments policy, it offers no clues on the amount of money leaving your firm at any given time. Obviously, this can lead to unforeseen cash flow problems.

To get a better fix on your cash outflow, multiply the value of each payable item by its age in days. Then, at the end of the period, total the days payable and divide by the amount payable to obtain the velocity of your payables for the period.

The example on the next page illustrates several points. First, it is taking the company an average of 23.5 days to pay each dollar of bills. Thus, payments seem to be timely but not unduly early, conserving cash flow. Management should also relate the velocity rate to its production schedule to determine the extent to which inventories are being financed by suppliers. Also, it appears that payment of purchase order #3456 is late. The reason for the delay should be checked.

Purchase Order #	Amount Payables		Days Outstanding		Days Payable
6308	$2,300	x	15	=	$ 34,500
4102	$3,600	x	20	=	$ 72,000
5610	$4,200	x	19	=	$ 79,800
3456	$6,000	x	32	=	$192,000
	$16,100				$378,300

$$\frac{\$378{,}300}{\$16{,}100} = 23.5 \text{ payable velocity rate}$$

Speed Up Your Collections with EDTs

If your company uses a paper-based collections system, you can probably simplify your collection procedures, reduce the time it takes for the funds to reach your company and save money by connecting to a system using electronic depository transfers (EDTs).

Both the paper-based and electronic systems operate under the same general principles. Usually, collections are forwarded to a number of strategically located field depository banks. A third party (either agents of the main bank or a deposit reporting service) gathers information on the deposits and, at the right time, forwards that information to the main bank. Then the main bank transfers the funds out of the field depository bank and into the central account, where they are made available to the firm.

Here is where the systems differ: In an EDT system, the transfers are made electronically while a paper-based system uses depository transfer checks (DTCs). Consider the following:

- **Quick availability**
  With an EDT collection system, you can be sure that your funds will be available to you in 1 business day. With conventional DTCs, it may take 2 days or even longer for your funds to become available.
- **Lower costs**
  EDTs also have a clear edge in costs. Wire transfers, which are used extensively in DTC collection systems, cost $10 to $25 per transaction

Observation

Virtually every bank and financial institution are now part of the Automated Clearing House—at latest count there were more than 13,000 members in the nationwide network. Now they are moving strongly onto the Internet for commerce, bill payment and presentment, financial electronic data interchange, cross-border transactions, electronic checks and electronic benefits transfer. Nevertheless, you may find that your DTC system already meets your company's needs. If 1-day availability holds no particular advantage for your company, you may not wish to endure the confusion and expense involved in a changeover to an EDT system.

when both sending and receiving bank charges are considered. Prices for EDTs vary from bank to bank but average 4 cents per item.

- **Predictability**

  Other than quick access to your funds, the big advantage of EDTs is their uniformity. You are just about guaranteed 1-day availability, so you do not need to monitor your collection procedures as closely as in a paper-based system.

3
Up-To-Date Cash Management Techniques

Cash management at many companies mainly consists of firefighting. Only when cash shortages begin to appear does it become a subject of interest. Often, it is too late by then. A better strategy is to make cash management a regular exercise, part of your strategic planning. Managing your company's cash flow involves checking on all the company's operations. There is no better way to make sure your company is in good shape and to spot any signs of ill health before it develops into a raging fever.

Conduct a Cash Management Audit

An audit need not be difficult or time-consuming. Many firms can complete the process in 2 weeks. At the end of this period, you should know (1) how effective your present systems are; (2) whether you are using any questionable practices; (3) where your risks lie; and (4) what changes, if any, are needed to improve cash controls.

To conduct your audit, first gather all information on how cash moves through the company. This includes copies of recent bank statements, account analysis reports, daily cash worksheets and monthly or weekly cash management reports. Then set up a schedule for interviewing all employees involved in handling cash, ranging from the treasurer to clerical personnel. Find out what each job entails, why each job is handled in a particular way and whether the employee believes the job could be done more effectively.

In conducting the interviews, draw up a simple flowchart, along with a written description showing how money moves through the firm. Check back with employees to make sure your impressions and the flowchart are accurate. Then you will be ready to make recommendations, derived largely from your interviews.

Here are some key points to remember when you attempt to improve any cash management system:

Collections

If you do not use a lockbox system, check to see if one would pay for itself. For many firms, it does. How quickly do you send out invoices? Sending invoices the same day is always the goal. Be certain your discounts for quick payments, if any, are in line with your competitors' discounts. Check to see how much unearned discounts are costing you. If necessary, demand full payment from customers who take discounts without paying early. Do you assess penalties for late accounts? If not, why not?

Take a look at your record in screening out bad credit risks. Make sure your bad-debt ratio is getting better rather than worse.

Payments

First, set up a policy prescribing certain times when payments should be mailed to vendors. If one already exists, perhaps you should stretch out mailing times from, for example, 30 to 35 days. Be certain that it is company policy to take discounts. Use a zero-balance account to maximize cash flow whenever possible. You may also be able to save time and money by using your bank's account-reconciliation service.

Bank relations

Are you paying your bank by fee or with compensating balances? If it is with balances, you might want to consider a change. If it is with fees, be sure you are not being charged a premium.

Check around to see if you are receiving competitive availability on deposited checks. If you use a lockbox system, get your bank to provide you with timely information on deposits. Is your lockbox cost-effective? Arrange to receive monthly account analysis reports from your bank, and make sure that they are comprehensible.

Investments

Set up written guidelines on the quality and maturity of corporate investments to keep risk low. Always shop around for the best rates. Get your bank to provide you with balances early enough to permit effective investing.

Compile Cash Flow Projections

Although traditional long-term cash forecasts have been too complicated and imprecise for most small business owners, there is a newer format that overcomes most of these problems. The newer format provides a specific forecast of cash balances under different assumptions, and it is relatively easy to prepare.

The forecast is based on information in the cash flow statement mandated by the Financial Accounting Standards Board (FASB). You can divide the actual preparation into three basic steps:

1. **Establishing historical patterns**

   To make useful projections, you must first find out what your company's cash flow patterns have been in the past. The easiest yardstick to use is to treat the variables as a percentage of sales. Do this by first digging out your financial statements for the past 3 to 5 years. Pull the balance sheet and income statement categories needed to prepare a cash flow statement. Then convert each item into a percentage of sales.

   If the year-to-year fluctuations in the percentage of sales calculations are minor, you have already established your pattern. However, chances are the fluctuations will vary too widely to be useful in some categories.

   For example, cyclical swings in the economy may have affected your receivables/sales calculations, or a change in policy could have thrown your inventory/sales pattern out of whack.

   In such cases, the solution is to begin with a fixed amount of the element in question and add a percentage of sales to that. These sales amounts can easily be determined through linear regression, which is a widely used computer-based technique found in almost all financial management software programs.

Illustration

By using linear regression analysis, you determine that the percentage of sales patterns for selected categories in your company's financial statements are outlined as follows:

Category	Amount ($ million)	Plus percent of sales
Cash	0	2
Cost of Goods Sold	0	80
Selling, General and Administrative Expenses	14	5
Accounts Receivable	4	15
Inventories	10	15
Accounts Payable	0	8
Net Fixed Assets	30	20

2. Making financial statement projections

Next, use your percentage of sales guidelines to complete projections for selected balance sheet and income statement items. To do this, you must come up with a sales forecast. To cover all bases, take your best available sales forecast and then surround it with best case/worst case assumptions. That way, you will be prepared no matter what the future may bring.

Illustration

Your sales department is looking forward to a banner year, expecting a 15 percent sales jump over the $300 million in the previous year. You use a worst-case assumption of 5 percent sales growth (to $315 million) and a best case of a 25 percent gain (to $375 million). The Income Statement and Balance Sheet Projections Worksheet on the next page shows how your statement projections would look, using the percentages in the previous illustration:

Income Statement and Balance Sheet Projections				
Selected Account	**Actual 2007**		**Projected 2008**	
		low	**mid**	**high**
Income Statement ($ Million) Net Sales	300	315	350	375
Less:				
Cost of Goods Sold	240	252	280	300
Selling, General and Administrative Expenses	29	30	32	33
Depreciation	3	4	4	4
Net Income from Operations	28	29	34	38
Less:				
Interest Expense	2	3	3	3
Taxes	13	13	15	17
Net Income	13	13	16	18
For Dividends	8	8	8	8
For Retained Earnings	5	5	8	10
Balance Sheet ($ Million) Cash	6	6	7	8
Accounts Receivable	49	51	57	60
Inventories	55	57	63	66
Accounts Payable	24	25	28	30
Net Fixed Assets	90	93	100	105

3. Projecting cash balances

Once you forecast the financial statement balances, it is a simple matter to use the balances to compile cash flow projections. the Cash Flow Projection Worksheet on the next page shows how a projected cash flow statement would look, using the forecasts in the earlier example:

Cash Flow Projections ($ million)

	Actual 2007	Projected 2008		
Forecast Category		low	mid	high
Cash Flow from Operations*	31	33	38	42
Changes in Working Capital	2	3	11	16
Cash Internally Generated	33	36	49	58
Less: Capital Expenses	3	3	10	15
Dividends	8	8	8	8
Net Increase in Cash	22	25	31	35

*Net income from operations plus depreciation.

The firm winds up with a healthy cash position. A sizable dividend increase might be in order. However, because of internal leverage, the cash position rises disproportionately on higher sales.

Just-in-Time Cash Management Via EDI

First there was just-in-time (JIT) inventory management. Then came just-in-time cash management–or payment via electronic funds transfer–which also can be beneficial for some small companies. Certain companies have made the electronic data interchange (EDI), as it is formally called, the preferred method of settling intercompany transactions.

A small company can gain from using EDI in several ways. First, EDI is accurate, speedy and cheaper than paper transactions, so a switch to EDI will trim your billing and record keeping costs. Second, EDI allows companies to manage cash much more efficiently. When an electronic order is received, the system immediately sets a shipping and payment date. This allows firms to keep inventories to a minimum and accurately forecast cash needs weeks in advance.

Observation

If you are interested in converting to an electronic payment system, the technology is available and you need not make a major investment. All that is required is a personal computer with a modem. Your financial institution will do the rest. Even if the local bank does not handle electronic payments, it almost certainly maintains a correspondent relationship with a bank that does. You could then work through the correspondent bank's system.

You may have no choice about being a participant in electronic funds transfer (EFT) even if you do not want to convert to a fully electronic payment system now. Many states require companies to submit corporate tax payments via EFT.

Some Added Benefits of EFT

Many companies pay their employees via EFT. Why should you want to do that and thus lose several days of float? For one thing, EFT costs less than check writing: There is no printing, preparation, distribution and reconciliation. The cost savings may make up for the lost float.

In addition, EFT generally is more accurate than check writing, with less chance of error. Your company would not have to worry about correcting errors, to say nothing of the aggravation involved with replacing lost or stolen checks. Finally, direct deposit saves productivity time: You would not lose a worker's time because the employee is in a bank line trying to deposit a check.

From the employee's point of view, EFT is a big help. The worker gets paid even while sick or on vacation. Confidentiality is assured and there is less lost time. So your company will benefit from increased employee morale at the same time you save money via EFT.

Beyond payrolls, EFT can help your corporate operations. Cash concentration, as it is known, may enable your company to move funds swiftly from outlying locations to a central bank account, effectively increasing your available cash. Of course, if you can get your customers to hook up with your EFT system, you will receive payments immediately. Many federal agencies make payments directly to contractors and vendors under the government's Vendor Express program.

The costs of participating in EFT vary widely, depending on your area and the volume of your transactions. Companies save anywhere from 10 to 23 cents per payment each time they handle a transaction electronically, due to administrative cost savings, according to estimates by the National Automated Clearing House Association. Counting employee productivity (that is, time not spent in bank lines), the cost saving jumps to $1 to $1.35 per transaction.

For more information on EDI, visit the Website of the Uniform Code Council at *www.uc-council.org*.

Part II

Credit & Collections

4
Top Management's Role in Controlling Credit & Collections

No matter how competent your managers, credit and collections are areas that require your closest attention. The precise controls you will need for your operations depend on the specific situation in our own company. But here are some you will want to consider:

- An appropriate and enforced credit policy.
- More frequent and comprehensive receivables reports, with special emphasis on size and condition.
- Top management approval of credit limits for new customers and increases for older ones. (If you do not have credit limits established, your policy should require approval of initial orders from new customers and from older accounts that would result in granting substantially higher amounts of credit.)
- Notification of top management when there is any change in the payment record of an account, especially shifts from prompt to overdue payments.
- Efficient and effect collection procedures.
- Periodic test checks of your firm's credit and collection files.
- A trained collection staff.

The Search for Solutions

What to do to cope with the problem, and how to do it, are the big questions. Aside from the outright credit angle, finding the answers involves several complex issues:

- Determining the appropriate balance between inventory and receivables.
- Weighing the potential profits to be gained by extending credit against risks inherent in overblown accounts receivable.
- Whether and to what extent to clamp down on credit, depending on the economic and competitive climate.
- How to implement tough decisions that are unpalatable to the trade in face of competitors' practices without risking business suicide.

Your starting point must be an objective re-examination of your current credit practices. A firm's senior executives often are unaware of when unsound credit practices and policies creep into the company's operation. As a minimal defense, prudent executives are rebuilding their organizational strengths and capabilities and adopting additional safeguards.

The price of safety really is eternal vigilance in this case, especially because such a large share of your company's assets are out of your hands, on loan to your customers.

Observation

Some highly successful firms have found it helpful to have accounts receivable reports translated into running charts on which succeeding months' results can be added. The graphic presentation helps them spot changes quickly–before a slowdown in collections can have a serious impact on cash flow.

No business person can know how sound, or unsound, a firm's credit picture is until it has been tested. Until then, the prudent executive must assume that top-heavy trade credit is a serious problem. Such a situation presents a potential danger not only to current cash flow but to the very life of the company.

Spot-Check Your Present Practices

We advise repeated spot-checks of current credit and collection procedures. These will help you implement any tightening up of receivables that you decide is warranted. The spot-checks may also uncover some surprises that need immediate attention.

Repeat the spot-checks at the end of the month over the next few months to get quick feedback on whether the situation is getting worse, staying the same or improving.

The sections that follow are filled with tested and effective credit and collections policies and procedures. Use them to hone your own operations. Even a slight improvement in these vital areas can have a sizable positive impact on your cash flow.

5 Managing Customer Credit to Maximize Cash Flow

The old axiom:

"A sale is not a sale until the cash is in the bank"

has never been truer than it is today. The timely conversion of accounts receivable has become a matter of the highest concern for most firms.

The ultimate decisions on when to grant credit, how much to extend and how to collect past-due bills usually belong to top management, particularly in smaller firms that cannot afford the luxury of a full-blown credit department or an experienced credit manager. In normal times, rising sales can often mask deficiencies in your credit and collection policies. However, when business conditions worsen, the combination of sliding sales and aging receivables can put a serious dent in much-needed cash flow.

In this section we will explore credit policy and credit evaluation criteria and provide information vital to sound decision making. The opening pages discuss the need for an overall credit policy to act as a cornerstone for the credit and collection activities of your firm. Then we examine guidelines that can be used for evaluating current and potential customers' creditworthiness. Next, we look at methods for establishing lines of credit and setting appropriate limits. Finally, we discuss ways of measuring the effectiveness of your credit operation.

Establishing an Appropriate Credit Policy

In most firms, the credit department is considered as a sort of lone wolf operation–one that has little bearing on the overall goals and policies of the firm. As a result, credit policies are seldom coordinated to achieve the greatest possible benefit for the firm. Still, an overly rigid credit policy can thwart a company's sales goals; too liberal a stance can undermine any attempt to manage capital effectively.

A sound credit policy can prevent such clashes. By coordinating credit activities with sales and production objectives, you stand a much better chance of reaching the company's goals.

Take a Look at Your Industry

No credit policy can survive long if it strays very far afield from industry practices. However, within certain confines, you can set your policy to give your firm the maximum competitive edge. Even if credit usually is not used as a sales tool in your industry, your company may want to employ it to gain a leg up on its rivals. There are, however, several factors to take into consideration:

Your company's market position. A company with a dominant position in its market can sometimes afford to demand a bit more from its customers. By the same token, a new company may well use liberal credit terms as an inducement while building up its customer list.

Customer Type

Always keep your customer's financial needs in mind when setting credit policy. If, for instance, your principal customers are in a business that suddenly becomes short of capital, lower your sights to accommodate them. Otherwise you will lose market share. By contrast, if the industry that you serve is well capitalized, marginal customers could be asked to provide additional security, such as a personal guarantee or an interest-bearing note. (See pages 85.)

Observation

The vast majority of firms lie somewhere in between, fighting to maintain or expand market share. Thus, your firm's marketing strategy should have an important influence on credit policy. A volume-based marketing strategy calls for a liberal credit policy. However, selling big-ticket items to a small customer base requires a restrictive policy.

Merchandising Characteristics

The type of merchandise that your firm sells will influence your credit policy in a number of ways. Here are just a few of the factors that will enter into your decision on an appropriate credit policy:

Markup

If profit margins on your products are normally slim, your credit department will have to maintain strict standards just to make sure that bad debts are kept to a minimum. More risk can be taken on high-margin products since profits on paid accounts normally cover most bad-debt losses.

Prices

If your unit prices are low, you can usually get by with a uniform policy covering all your customers because the risk in actual dollars will not be that great on any one customer. On big-ticket items, however, one defaulted account can cause irreparable damage. Therefore, you should require a detailed analysis before extending credit.

Distribution Patterns

If you sell to a widely dispersed geographical area, there is little chance that you will ever know your customers very well. Therefore, credit approval must be carried out on a long-distance basis, possibly involving letters of credit (see page 43). Selling to a concentrated area lends itself more easily to quick credit approval and usually involves more intense competition. Here, the tendency is to loosen the credit reins.

Observation

While each of the factors discussed here will be an important influence on the overall credit policy of your firm, the vagaries of the business cycle could enter in as well. Obviously, when times are good, your customers will be in a better position to pay their debts. Thus, credit restrictions can be relaxed a bit if such action is deemed necessary. In sluggish periods, however, delayed payments become more common. Thus, you may be faced with the dilemma of needing to tighten credit restrictions when sales volume has already been dampened by the slowed economy. There is no ready answer to such a quandary, but you can ease the pain somewhat by keeping your credit policy flexible enough to cope with any sudden changes in the business outlook.

Financial Strength

Your company's financial strength should be a prime factor in setting credit policy. If you are under financed to begin with, you can ill afford a credit policy that can lead to losses. You can only afford to carry overdue accounts if you have financial resources large enough to withstand the drain on cash flow.

Choosing the Right Credit Policy

There are two basic components of a credit policy. The first involves the amount of risk your company is willing to take in granting credit to your customers. The second involves the amount of effort you are willing to put into the collection process itself.

There is a measuring rod for each component. Your credit analysis standards will largely determine the risk factor; the amount of money you spend on collection will determine its effectiveness.

Four broad categories emerge from joining the risk and effort components of credit policy. You can, of course, shade these policies in any number of ways, depending on the precise amount of risk and effort that your firm is willing to undertake. Nonetheless, whatever course you follow, you will probably decide to choose a variation on one of the following classifications:

1. **Tough acceptance/vigorous collection**
   This type of policy is suitable primarily for a firm with a well-entrenched market position operating in a fairly healthy business environment. In a less favorable climate, this policy can cost too much in sales. Risk analysis is thorough, probably involving more than just a credit bureau check. A fairly large collection staff is needed, but costs may be offset by improved receivables turnover and minimal bad-debt losses.
2. **Tough acceptance/easy collection**
   This type of policy concentrates primarily on good credit risks, assuming that they generally will pay their bills on time. However, this policy is most effective when a firm's cost of capital is low and customers are in a comfortable financial position.
3. **Easy acceptance/vigorous collection**
   This policy is commonly used by a firm seeking to expand market share in a competitive business climate. However, putting the entire

emphasis on collection can be costly. Firms with a high markup and low unit cost usually fare best with this type of policy.

4. **Easy acceptance/casual collection**
   Only firms with total emphasis on building unit volume should attempt to implement this policy. Margins should be high to cover inevitable bad-debt losses. Still, despite the risks, a few newly organized, high-tech firms have made this policy work for them.

Evaluating Customers' Creditworthiness

Your company may be asked to extend credit to a wide variety of customers. You may be serving large companies, small companies, partnerships, corporations, proprietorships, manufacturers, wholesalers, service companies and so forth.

The amount of credit information available on different types of companies can vary widely. Thus, while every company should be required to demonstrate that it is worthy of your credit, you will be using several channels to gather the necessary information to justify your decisions.

As a general rule, new accounts should be required, at the very minimum, to provide evidence of their financial viability through:

- A satisfactory credit rating by a commercial credit bureau, such as Dun & Bradstreet;
- bank and trade references; and
- timely financial statements.

Each of these sources of information is equally important and deserves separate consideration, which follows.

Using Commercial Credit Bureaus

By joining an area credit bureau you gain access not only to credit information about your local customers but also to facts about your more distant ones through a national network of credit bureaus. Credit bureaus are generally for-profit organizations that charge fees for membership and services.

Some credit bureaus specialize in one or two industries. Because of their limited focus, they are able to operate more economically than their broaderscope counterparts, so they often are cheaper. If most of your customers are concentrated in a few industries, find out from the industry associations whether there are special credit bureaus serving their industries.

Where to find a credit bureau: For further information about commercial credit bureaus, contact the National Association of Credit Management (NACM), 8815 Centre Park Dr., Suite 200, Columbia, MD 21045; phone (410) 740-5560; Website: *www.nacm.org*. This nonprofit trade association, which has 53 autonomous chapters throughout the United States with a total of 30,000 members, offers nationwide reporting and collection services.

There are four major business-information companies that can provide you with a credit report on a prospective customer: Dun & Bradstreet, (908) 665-5000; Equifax, (404) 885-8000; Experian, (888) 397-3742; and Trans Union, (800) 335-9888.

For example, Dun & Bradstreet Business Credit Services offers subscribers a full range of business information and credit advisory services on a contract basis. The company keeps tabs on hundreds of thousands of U.S. businesses. In addition to its well-known credit ratings, Dun & Bradstreet assigns payment-performance (PAYDEX) scores to the companies it follows. When compared with the average score of its industry, a company's PAYDEX score is a useful measure of the firm's ability to meet its obligations. Dun & Bradstreet also ranks a company's financial condition and business outlook in terms of industry averages. These rankings are handy tools for quickly assessing how stable a company is and what its future prospects may be.

Should you use a local industry credit bureau or a centralized business information service like Dun & Bradstreet? That depends on which credit reporting agency meets your needs at the lowest price. Shop around for the best deal.

What a credit bureau can and cannot do for you: Do not expect a credit bureau to make a judgment for you. Credit bureaus leave the evaluation up to their clients. They simply provide information through their ratings and reports:

- **Credit ratings consist of two elements.**
  The first tells you how strong the company is financially. The second gives an indication of the company's track record in paying its bills.

- **Credit reports are more detailed.**
  They include a summary of the most recent financial statements, a rundown on recent credit payments, a short history of the company and a report from the company's bank. The report also comments on the financial history of the company, its financial condition and the trend of the business.

In short, through its ratings and reports, a credit bureau can give you a pretty good idea of how a company has handled its bills, what its financial strengths currently are and whether business is improving or declining. For most credit departments, a check with a credit bureau is a necessary first step.

Do not end your search there, however. For one thing, credit bureau ratings and reports may be up to 18 months old. For another, they are sometimes inaccurate, especially when the company they are evaluating is new or small.

The Six C's of Credit

For generations, credit students have been told to look to the Six C's when granting credit. Old as they are, they still hold true today. If your customer ranks high on the Six C's, you can be almost certain that the bills will be paid on time. Here they are:

1. **Capital**
   Does the company have enough capital to pay your bill?
2. **Capability**
   Are the owners capable managers and do they know the business?
3. **Character**
   Can the owners be trusted and are they running a legitimate business?
4. **Circumstances**
   Are there any factors beyond the control of your firm and your customer's that could cause serious trouble down the line? A business downturn might be one example. A credit crunch might be another.
5. **Collateral**
   What tangible evidence do you have that the bill will be paid?
6. **Coverage**
   Is your customer's insurance coverage sufficient? If a disaster struck, would the policy cover the customer's obligation to you?

Checking Out Bank and Trade References

A favorable D&B report will tell you all you need to know about customers that are good credit risks. For those given a high D&B rating, you can usually extend credit without any further checks. However, in many cases, the data from the commercial credit bureau will be either inconclusive or insufficient. Here you will need additional information before making your decision.

To obtain the necessary information, contact your new customer, preferably in person. Thank him for the order, and then, stressing that the request is routine, ask for the name of the company's bank, several trade references and a copy of the company's most recent financial statements.

Caution

If your customer is reluctant to give you bank and trade references, watch out. This type of inquiry is common practice in most industries. A firm that hesitates to pass such information along might have something to hide.

Financial statements are another matter. Many firms prefer to keep their financial condition private in order not to give the competition an edge. So do not press the point. You can probably come to a decision by checking out references. If not, renew your request for financial statements later.

Reviewing the Bank Report

Your customer's bank can be a valuable source of information about the company's financial resources and bill-paying habits. Although banks are not required to provide you with credit information, most will cooperate if you approach them correctly. Make it clear to the bank that your mutual customer is aware of the credit inquiry. Unless there are time constraints, send your inquiry in writing–many banks are reluctant to give out customer information over the phone and some refuse to do so.

The National Association of Credit Management's standard inquiry form, Request for Bank Credit Information (Form 19), simplifies the process of checking a prospect's bank references. Form 19 asks the bank for information about the customer's account balances, the outstanding balances of the firm's bank loans and the company's loan payment record. It also provides space for the bank's lending officer to comment on the institution's experience with the customer. (If the company has done business with the bank for less than a year, ask the firm for the name of its previous bank.)

Form 19 can be obtained by contacting the NACM at (410) 740-5560. The forms are sold (prepaid) in quantities of 250 or 500. Your main goal in evaluating bank information is to find out whether the customer has enough ready cash to pay you on time. Consider the following issues:

- **Do the company's account balances seem in line with the size of its order?**
  If not, what is the reason? A low checking account balance may mean that the firm has skimpy resources. But it can also indicate that the firm is using the bank's cash management services, which place available balances in interest bearing investments.
- **Is the company making its loan payments on time?**
  Late payments usually indicate sluggish cash flow. If this is the case, you also might fall victim to delayed payments.
- **Are the customer's loans secured or unsecured?**
  If they are secured, this means that the bank has a lien on a portion of the firm's assets. If the company had to liquidate those assets to pay off debts, lenders with secured credit would be paid first and you could be left with an uncollectible credit obligation.
- **Does the bank's lending officer feel that the company's financial controls are adequate?**
  A here today, gone tomorrow customer is not a good risk.

Appraising Trade References

Always keep in mind that the trade references your customer supplies are bound to be those that show the firm in the best possible light. If these references do not check out well, your customer's credit record with other companies is probably sliding downhill. In particular, take a look at the amount of credit extended by other firms. If their balances with your new customer are close to the value of your order, you can probably expect to be paid on time. If, however, your order is several times as large as

Recommendation

If the customer has placed a much larger order with you than with other firms, cross-check other sources—the bank's report, the company's financial statement—to be sure the firm has the resources to pay you. Also, if the customer's business with the company you are querying took place some time ago, double-check to find out whether any changes in the company's business or financial status might adversely affect its ability to meet obligations.

the balances for the others, a prompt payment record does not mean very much.

Caution

Keep in mind that all credit information is given in confidence and should remain confidential. The disclosure of any of this information could very well shut off most, if not all, of your sources and could conceivably result in legal difficulties as well. Even if you decide to ask for a clarification from your customer, do not disclose the source of your information.

Evaluating Customers' Financial Statements

Theoretically, when you ask a customer for financial statements, you should receive an income statement and a balance sheet. Practically speaking, however, the income statement is likely to be out of date and useless for investigative purposes. Most companies prepare income statements once or twice each year, but quarterly balance sheets are common.

If you can obtain an up-to-date income statement, it will not require much additional work to come up with a complete picture of the company's state of affairs. Even without an income statement, however, you can learn a great deal.

Some, if not all, of the ratios shown below will be familiar. They are a relatively painless way of shedding light on a potential customer. (When using ratios that require sales figures, those for the latest available year will do.)

- **Current ratio: current assets ÷ current liabilities.**
  Ideally, a current ratio of 2.0 or better indicates an acceptable margin of safety.
- **Quick ratio: (cash + accounts receivable) ÷ current liabilities.**
  A quick ratio of 1.0 shows that there is $1 of liquid assets to cover every dollar of current debt. Normally considered the toughest test of financial strength, a quick ratio of 1.0 or better indicates adequate liquidity.
- **Current liabilities to net worth: current liabilities ÷ net worth.**
  This ratio indicates how much of your customer's equity capital would be needed to pay off all short-term debt obligations. The lower the ratio, the better. Generally, you should shy away from a firm with a ratio of 66 percent or higher.

- **Inventory turnover: cost of goods sold ÷ inventory.**
  This ratio measures the number of times that inventory is turned over each year. The trend is important. If the ratio keeps decreasing, your customer's inventories are probably excessive and draining needed cash. If the ratio suddenly rises, inventories may be too low, thus endangering production schedules.
- **Return on net worth: net after-tax income ÷ net worth.**
  Frequently dubbed return on equity, it is the acid test of a firm's profitability. If this ratio does not at least match the going T-bill rate, your customer might be better off using capital invested in the firm for some other purpose.
- **Average collection period: accounts receivable ÷ credit sales x 360.**
  This ratio will give you a good idea of how fast your customer is collecting bills. Usually, 35 days - 46 days is considered normal. Anything over 50 days may indicate sizable uncollectible accounts and should give you cause for concern. As an example, if a company with $20 million in annual credit sales maintained receivables of $2 million, the average collection period would be 36 days ($2,000,000 ÷ $20,000,000 x 360 = 36).

CCM Credit Scoring System

Some companies find the Commercial Credit Matrix (CCM) credit scoring system to be a useful tool for assessing a company's financial health. The system is fully explained in the booklet *Analyzing Financial Statements: Quick and Clean*, available from Books on Business. The CCM system uses data from the company's financial statement to calculate, and combine into a single numerical rating, five basic financial ratios: the current ratio; quick ratio; liquidity ratio–(cash + accounts receivable) ÷ current liabilities; equity/debt ratio (total equity ÷ total liabilities); and return on equity ratio (year's net income ÷ equity).

To obtain a perfect combined credit health rating of 20, a company would have to meet or exceed the following ratios and percentages:

- Current ratio: 2.15
- Quick ratio: 1.11
- Liquidity: 0.45
- Equity/debt: 2.01

- Return on equity: 15.6 percent

The credit cutoff point would be a CCM rating of 8. This financial health rating, developed by financial consultant James Kristy, can be fine-tuned to take other factors into account:

- Points can be added to the rating for guarantees or collateral to lessen the credit risk.
- Negative points may be assigned for a negative return on investment when a financial statement shows losses.
- A corollary probability of failure index also can be worked up from the same information to help you assess the chances of a customer going bankrupt. In addition, a formula that factors in the expected cost to your firm of a customer's potential failure can also be applied.
- A long-term debt matrix is provided for credit decisions that extend beyond a year or two. (The regular CCM is designed to measure a company's short-term debt capability.)

CCM can also be used as a planning aid and an early warning system for spotting potential financial problems in your own firm.

A software version of the matrix and scoring system is also available from Books on Business, 5482 Burlingame Ave., Buena Park, CA 90621; phone (714) 523-0357.

Determining Appropriate Credit Limits

In granting credit, apply the same yardstick to all your customers. Develop objective standards for setting credit limits, and enforce your credit terms equally and consistently. Not only is this good business practice; it is also a matter of law in the consumer-credit area.

Some companies index credit limits to their customers' credit rating: that is, those with a top rating receive unlimited credit or the top credit line, and the rest get limited credit in decreasing amounts, depending on where they fall on the ratings scale. Although this is a single and efficient way of assigning credit limits, it does not take into account qualitative factors, such as an upswing or downturn in sales, that might alter the customer's credit status.

A more flexible approach is to set your own criteria for credit judgments, then rank your customers in terms of how well they measure up to your standards.

This way, you can integrate into your credit evaluation system all the factors you consider important for the welfare of your business and the effectiveness of your credit policy.

Recommendation

If you have so many customers that a point system becomes cumbersome, consider putting your personal computer to work to do the credit evaluation. You may be able to find software that meets your needs. Or, you could hire a computer programmer to design the program for you and, from time to time, update it as your requirements change.

The chart on page 78 gives examples of the criteria you can use to evaluate your customers and lists a sampling of sources where you can find information relevant to each criterion. The numerical point system it uses is a simple way to sort out your customers. You would grant credit to customers scoring zero and above, increasing the amount of credit as you went up the scale. For example, you might decide to offer unlimited credit to your top two categories–customers scoring 11 or 12–and limited credit in various amounts for those scoring 0 to 10. You'd deny credit to customers with a minus score unless they could offer a solid guarantee or security to back their borrowing.

Once you decide that a new customer has the wherewithal to pay bills on time, you must then decide how much credit to extend. Usually, the first order is approved immediately, provided that it does not exceed certain guidelines. One widely used rule of thumb is to fill any first order up to 10 percent of the customer's net worth. After that, a formal line of credit is opened. Once approved, this line of credit should be exceeded only upon approval of top management.

Methods for Setting Credit Lines

There are a number of methods you can use to set credit lines. The choice depends on your personnel, your industry and your customer. In all likelihood, you will find one or a combination of several of the methods below suitable for your firm:

Requirements Credit Line

This type of credit line should be reserved for your most substantial customers. It simply means that your firm will extend credit for any order that is placed, no matter how large. Another version, called a normal requirements line, permits credit for all the customer's normal purchases–usually with a 10 percent allowable increase. Again, this type of credit line should be extended only to customers with particularly good credentials.

Rating-Based Credit Line

Many firms simply use D&B ratings as a basis for establishing credit lines. Customers with top D&B ratings could, for instance, be put on a requirements basis, with the others scaled down from, say, $10,000 to a minimum of a few hundred dollars, depending on the ratings.

Order-Based Credit Line

This type of credit line places a limit on orders–either by number or by dollar amount. It is particularly useful for a decentralized company that accepts customer's orders at a number of locations. There are two ways of handling it:

- **Dollar-based order limits**
  This method places a limit on the dollar amount of any order that can be handled without prior credit approval. Some companies place order limits for all customers, merely as a secondary credit check.
- **Time limits on orders**
  You can also limit the total amount of orders that can be placed in any given time period without prior approval. Monthly allowances are usually established, but you can stretch the time period out to 3 months or even 6 months if necessary.

Credit Evaluation Criteria

Criterion	Assessment	Points	Sources of Information
Financial Condition	strong	+1	Credit Ratings
	Moderate	0	Credit Reports
	Weak	-1	Company's Financial Statement
			Bank Reports
Financial Condition Compared with Industry	Strong	+1	Dun & Bradstreet Credit Guide and Analysis Report
	Moderate	0	Dun & Bradstreet Industry Norms and Key Business Ratios Report

	Weak	-1	U.S. Department of Commerce Survey of Current Business
Overall Payment Performance	Prompt	+1	Credit Ratings
	Average	0	Credit Reports
	Slow	-1	Bank Reports
			Trade References
Business Payments Performance Compared with Industry	Superior	+1	Dun & Bradstreet Payment Analysis Report
	Equal	0	Dun & Bradstreet PAYDEX
	Below par	-1	U.S. Department of Commerce Survey of Current Business
Loan Payment Performance	Prompt	+1	Bank Reports
	Average	0	
	Slow	-1	
Trends in the Company's Business	Upward	+1	Credit Reports
	Stable	0	Company's Financial Statements
	Downward	-1	Dun & Bradstreet Credit Guide and Analysis Report
Industry Trends	Upward	+1	U.S. Department of Commerce Data
	Stable	0	The Business Press
	Downward	-1	
Management Capability	Excellent	+2	Credit Reports
	Good	+1	Bank Reports
	Fair	0	Better Business Bureau
	Poor	-1	Trade References
Collateral for Credit	Ample	+1	
	Adequate	0	Credit Reports

	Inadequate	-1	
Insurance	Ample	+1	Company's Insurance Carrier
	Adequate	0	Credit Reports
	Inadequate	-1	
Years in Business	More than 7	+1	Credit Reports
	4-7	0	
	Less than 4	-1	

Using a Formula-Based System

Formula-based credit systems have a large advantage over other methods of setting credit lines because they force management to use the same parameters for all the company's customers. Nevertheless, most formula systems are too rigid to be useful and fail to consider the quality of a customer's financial underpinnings. However, with computers doing most of the work, formula systems that eliminate most of these objections have been developed.

One such system is currently being used by a large metals processing company. The firm bases its credit decision on two elements. First, it establishes a basic credit line by rating the customer on four separate financial ratios. Then it uses information developed in a desirability profile to adjust the basic line.

You might want to adapt its system for your own use. Here's how it works:

Establishing the Basic Credit Line

The table on page 83 (Financial Risk Profile) illustrates how customers are classified according to four separate financial ratios. The first two ratios are used to determine liquidity; the second two indicate whether the customer's financial policies have been sound.

Your customer's final ranking will depend on its poorest performance among the four. For instance, suppose your customer's current ratio, quick ratio and current debt/net worth all fell into the good category. If the final ratio, or total debt/net worth, worked out to 1.75, your customer would be classified as a limited risk, despite receiving a good ranking in the other three categories. Accordingly, you would set its basic credit line at 9 percent of net worth or 18 percent of working capital, whichever was lower.

Developing the Desirability Profile

Part two of the formula calls for using a point score to test the quality of your customer's credit history. The fewer points, the better. The needed information can be obtained from credit reports, bank references or the observations of your own salespeople. Here are the factors:

- **Payment history**
  Mostly prompt–2; Fair–4; Mostly slow–6.
- **Product profitability**
  High–1; Average–2; Below average–3.
- **Management evaluation**
  Above average–2; Average–4; Below average–6.
- **Competition**
  Heavy–1; Average–2; Below average–3.
- **Years in business**
  Over seven–1; Four to seven–2; Less than four–3.
- **Bank borrowing**
  Unsecured–2; Secured by fixed assets–4; Secured by current assets–6.
- **Analyst's assessment**
  Comfortable–0; Uncomfortable–3; Very uncomfortable–6.
- **Need for customer's business**
  Great–6; Average–12; Small–6-18.

Observation

At first glance, the point distribution rating the need for a customer's business might seem arbitrary. However, if the sale is imperative, the need alone justifies a lower score. If the sale is not really needed, you are likely to keep other standards high. You are most likely to lower your guard on sales that meet an average need.

The point score determines the weight, or multiplier, for your customer's basic credit line. You would multiply the basic line of a customer with the best possible point score (15-17 points) by the highest weight of 4.0. The multiplier for the worst point score (43-45 points) would be 0.25, reducing the line to one-fourth its original size. A neutral score of 30-32 points would receive a 1.0 multiplier, resulting in no change. You can set your own multipliers between these extremes, depending on the conditions in your own industry and credit experience.

Z-Scores: Another Alternative

The Z-score was originally developed as a tool to predict insolvency. Widely used by banks and other lending institutions to rate a company's finances, the system offers yet another way to evaluate a customer's financial health and stability, using nothing more than a recent balance sheet and income statement.

The system is based on five ratios, each of which is weighted according to its importance as an indicator of financial health. Here's a rundown of the ratios, their weights and how they are used:

1. **Working Capital ÷ Total Assets x 1.2**
   This ratio uses current assets minus current liabilities to measure liquidity, or the ability to meet current obligations.
2. **Retained Earnings ÷ Total Assets x 1.4**
   Here, the ratio gives an indication of the profitability of the company over time.
3. **Operating Profits ÷ Total Assets x 3.3**
   This is your return on assets, a commonly used measure of profitability. Note the weighting.
4. **Sales ÷ Total Assets x 1.0**
   The weight is neutral on this yardstick for gauging how many sales dollars are generated by each dollar of assets.
5. **Equity Value ÷ Total Liabilities x 0.6**
   This ratio measures the volatility of the company's capital structure. Use the market value of the common stock, where possible; book value can be substituted. Do not forget to add the liquidating value of any preferred stock outstanding. Unlike the other ratios, this one is negatively weighted.

Financial Risk Profile				
Rating	Good	Fair	Limited	Marginal
Current Ratio	Over 2.00	2.00-1.63	1.62-1.25	Under 1.25
Quick Ratio	Over 1.00	1.00-0.76	0.75-0.50	Under 0.50
Current Debt/ Net Worth	Under 0.75	0.75-1.00	1.01-1.25	Over 1.25
Total Debt/Net Worth	Under 1.25	1.25-1.62	1.63-2.00	Over 2.00
Credit Line You'll Grant				
% Net Worth	15%	12%	9%	6%
% Working Capital	30%	24%	18%	12%

Balance Sheet (in $000)		
Current Assets	$600	
Fixed and Other Assets	$510	
Total Assest		$1,100
Current Liabilities	$290	
Long-Term Debt	$220	
Total Liabilities		$510
Common Stocks	$110	
Capital Surplus	$140	
Retained Earnings	$340	
Shareholder's Equity		$590
Total Liabilites		$1,100
Income Statement (in $000)		
Sales	$1,200	
Operating Profit		$95

Observation

There are definite cutoff points in Z-scores. For instance, a total score of 3.0 or better indicates that the company is in sound financial shape. Indeed, anything above 2.7 means that the company is likely to survive. A score below 2.0 implies that some problems exist. The problems could be serious if it falls below 1.8. A negative score supposedly foreshadows imminent bankruptcy.

The Z-score calculations would look like this:

(1) 310 ÷ 1,100 x 1.2 = 0.34

(2) 340 ÷ 1,100 x 1.4 = 0.43

(3) 95 ÷ 1,100 x 3.3 = 0.29

(4) 1,200 ÷ 1,100 x 1.0 = 1.09

(5) 590 ÷ 510 x 0.6 = 0.69

Total Z-score = 2.84

Illustration

A new customer applying for a sizable credit line supplies financial statements containing the information to the left.

Your customer's Z-score stands well above the 2.7 mark and is not far below the 3.0 mark for very sound firms. In other words, the company is in good shape financially and worthy of credit.

Yet Another Way to Test: The H-Score

While the Z-score is used to test the financial stability of mostly large firms, there's also the H-score, a newer statistical model that measures the financial health of small companies. Both the H- and the Z-score models evaluate a company's financial health by applying weights to a group of widely used financial ratios and then adding up the results. The way in which ratios are weighted becomes the critical factor in determining the accuracy of the model.

For the H-score method, three business professors and one portfolio manager devised weights for each of nine financial ratios by analyzing the financial ratios of 120 small companies whose total assets were under $10 million. Some of those companies went bankrupt while others succeeded. In a test, the model correctly predicted bankruptcy for 98 percent of the failed companies 1 year prior to their demise, and for 81 percent of the failed firms 2 years prior to their bankruptcy.

While the H-score model is used by banks to determine the creditworthiness of small firms, you can use the method to determine the health of customers and suppliers.

The analysis itself requires nothing more than a balance sheet and an income statement for the company under review, plus a calculator with a logarithm (log) key.

To determine a company's stability, multiply each of the nine ratios by its assigned weight. Then add the individual ratio scores together to obtain a total H-score. A total score of 1.0 or better indicates that the company is in sound financial shape. Any result below 1.0 implies that some problems exist. The lower the score, the more serious the problems.

Here are the H-score weights that are assigned to each financial ratio:

1. **Retained Earnings ÷ Total Assets x 5.5**
   This ratio measures the profitability of the company over time. As a result, it has a high weighting.

2. **Sales ÷ Total Assets x 0.2**
   The asset turnover ratio illustrates the capability of the firm's assets to generate sales.
3. **Pretax Earnings ÷ Equity x 0.7**
   Use book equity in this common calculation for measuring return on equity.
4. **Cash Flow ÷ Total Debt x 1.3**
   This can be a crucial indicator of a small firm's ability to weather a downturn.
5. **Debt ÷ Total Assets x –0.1**
   The higher the debt ratio, the greater the possibility of bankruptcy. Thus, the weighting is negative.
6. **Current Liabilities ÷ Total Assets x 2.3**
   This leverage ratio measures the firm's ability to use assets to meet obligations as they come due.
7. **Log of Total Tangible Assets x 0.6**
   The first of two logarithmic calculations, this measures the size of the firm.
8. **Working Capital ÷ Total Debt x 1.1**
   Shrinking working capital can spell trouble for a small firm, particularly if debt is high.
9. **Log of EBIT ÷ Interest x 0.9**
   This is the familiar interest coverage ratio, with the log of earnings before interest and taxes (EBIT) used to keep the weighting in line.

> **Caution**
>
> The H-score should not be used as the sole basis for evaluating the creditworthiness of another firm. It offers valuable insight but should always be combined with other forms of credit checks and analysis.

Securing Marginal Accounts

There will, of course, be times when your credit check indicates that the potential customer should not be granted credit in the usual business sense. After all, very few customers that fall below your credit standards will be able to pay cash. Still, do not reject the order out of hand. There are steps you can take to secure the account and make it collectible. Here are some of the more common methods:

Short-Term Notes

Most firms use short-term notes when a payment record has been slow but without any bad debts. In brief, a note is a legal instrument that gives the customer a specified amount of time to pay the bill and charges interest after that. The note must be signed by an officer of the customer's firm.

> **Recommendation**
>
> If you are still in doubt about the note, ask a principal of the firm to add a personal guarantee. In some states, you can even use a judgment note, which permits you to get a quick court judgment upon default.

Letters of Guarantee

A letter of guarantee is simply a legally worded document guaranteeing payment of the account in question. When using a letter of guarantee, always make certain that the guarantor has a good credit rating and the wherewithal to pay your account. There are several types of guarantees:

- **Personal guarantee**
  By far the most common, this type includes a guarantee by an officer or a principal of the firm involved, indicating that he will be personally responsible if the payment is not made.
- **Parent-firm guarantee**
  If your customer is a subsidiary of a larger, more creditworthy firm, you can usually obtain a guarantee from the parent company.
- **Outside-firm guarantee**
  Sometimes, if your customer is an important supplier to a larger firm, that firm will guarantee your customer's account. In this case you should be sure to check out the guarantor's credit rating first.

Letters of Credit

The best security you can get for an uncertain account is a letter of credit (L/C). This document, issued by a bank, guarantees that payment will be made if certain conditions (usually delivery terms) specified in the letter are met. Because the bank is, in effect, substituting its credit standing for your customer's when it issues you a letter of credit, you can be sure that payments will be made promptly.

Letters of credit come in many forms. Each is tailor-made to suit the transaction, with the purchaser (opener) usually dictating the delivery terms and the seller (beneficiary) normally setting the terms of payment. Even though they are customized, all letters of credit have certain terms in common:

- **Revocable or irrevocable**
  An irrevocable letter of credit has a fixed expiration date and cannot be canceled or altered before that time without the agreement of all parties. A revocable letter of credit can be canceled at any time. As you might expect, revocable letters of credit are useless for business purposes and are rarely used.
- **Confirmed or unconfirmed**
  Frequently, in a long-distance transaction, a bank issuing a letter of credit will ask a correspondent bank in the seller's area to guarantee payment to the seller. In this case a double guarantee exists, and the seller's local bank is said to have confirmed the letter of credit. The confirming bank has an irrevocable obligation to fund the letter when all the terms have been satisfied.

Caution

Business owners generally regard letters of credit as an almost foolproof way to ensure payment in a long-distance transaction or from a customer with a sketchy credit history. Studies have shown, however, that up to half of all L/Cs issued are faulty in one way or another, which means that their guarantees are useless. Most L/C problems revolve around the requirement that the seller submit certain documents to receive payment and ensure a fair transaction. In some instances, the bank, the buyer or both might include conditions that are difficult for the seller to meet. As a result, companies running into documentation snags face the risk of delayed payment at best, or no payment at worst.

L/C users can take these steps to reduce the possibility of documentation problems:

- **Read the fine print**
  Scrutinize the L/C carefully and then call the issuing bank before you ship the goods. You will be looking for answers to two questions: (1) Can you provide the documentation required under the letter of credit? (2) Are there any hidden requirements?
- **Centralize document control**
  One big reason for L/C snags is that discrepancies occur when different persons handle different documents. For one transaction, various documents might come from a sales department, a shipping section and a forwarder. When so many people handle documents, the chances for an error multiply. Keep in mind that it does not have to be a major mistake; a simple spelling error or a late filing can be enough to negate the L/C guarantee.

Recommendation

You should assign a single person the responsibility for gathering all the needed documentation in proper form. This person should know, in advance of the shipment, exactly what documents are needed, where to obtain them and when to present them.

Establishing Credit Terms

Payment terms are closely bound to marketing strategies, so consult your sales representatives or marketing manager before setting up payment schedules. They will fill you in on what their customers expect, and this often depends on payment patterns in the customers' industries.

For instance, if a customer's industry norm is payment within 15 days after delivery, do not lose sales by requiring payment upon delivery unless the customer has proved to be a deadbeat in the past (and then you might be better off requiring C.O.D. terms).

Nevertheless, always insist on payment within 30 days of delivery at the latest since you will have to pay most of your own bills within this time frame. This is standard business procedure. It is also the only way you will keep your accounts receivable in balance with your cash flow. You might also:

Offer a Discount for Early Payment

While the 30-day turnaround is adequate, the sooner your customers pay you, the more brisk your cash flow will be. So encourage them to pay you early. One way to do this is by offering a discount based on your company's cost of capital. The amount of the discount will vary directly with how early the customer pays the bill. (See page 108 for details.)

Charge Interest on Late Payments

Likewise, discourage your customers from paying you late by charging daily interest on the overdue balance. The interest rate can also be based on your company's cost of capital. This will offset your cost of borrowing money to cover the overdue bills.

When you offer early-payment discounts or charge late-payment penalties, state your terms clearly in the original contract. Set them off conspicuously in bold type so that your customers will be aware of your payment policies. Do not let customers claim more of a discount than they have earned, and do not waive interest charges for favored customers. Special credit treatment of favored customers can, in effect, lower the cost of your goods or services for these customers. This is unfair to the rest of your customers.

Measure the Effectiveness of Your Credit Policy

Once a credit policy has been established, you should develop some procedure to monitor its effectiveness. There are two common yardsticks for measuring credit activity today. Both give valuable insight into credit operations but also have definite limitations:

Measuring Your Mistakes

The first, the ratio of bad debts to sales, measures your credit mistakes, so to speak. If this ratio is higher than your industry norm, it tells you that your credit policies are too liberal. However, it says nothing about troublesome receivables that are aging but have not yet reached the bad-debt stage.

Using the Flow-of-Funds Calculation

This method of calculating the speed of your collections is carried out in two steps:

Step 1. Gather the information

There are only two pieces of information needed to determine your flow-of-funds rate: the age (in days) of the invoice being paid and the amount of the payment. Both can be obtained from the employee handling the payments, or your computer can be programmed to provide the data.

Step 2. Make the calculation

Multiply the value of each invoice by its age in days. When you reach the end of the period (usually a month, but it can be every 15 days if desired), total the flow-of-funds and divide by dollars received. This provides the flow-of-funds rate (or the velocity of your collections) for the period.

If you collect in less than the time you've set in your credit terms, your collection activities are satisfactory. But if it takes longer than your set terms, you need to tighten credit standards.

Caution

The price differentials that result when you make exceptions to your discount and interest rules might violate the Robinson-Patman Act if your products are tangible goods. This statute, part of federal antitrust legislation, makes it illegal under certain conditions for a company to sell the same commodity to two or more U.S–based purchasers at different prices—particularly if the price differential could serve to lessen competition (among your customers) or create a monopoly (by underpricing your own competitors). The act, which does not govern services, applies to sales within a limited time frame (generally six months) that involve interstate commerce.

In the period reviewed in the table below, it took Jasper Corporation an average of 29.64 days to collect each dollar in receivables. Assuming that the terms set were net 30, Jasper is doing very well. If the flow-of-funds rate were 40 days or more, Jasper management might want to take remedial action.

Jasper Corporation Flow-of-Funds Calculation					
Invoice Number	Days Outstanding		Amount Paid		Flow-of-funds
3608	28	x	$1,200	=	$33,600
4517	18	x	4,300	=	77,400
2778	35	x	3,700	=	129,500
1898	42	x	2,800	=	109,200
	$\frac{349,700}{11,800}$		= 29.64 flow-of-funds rate		

Credit Department Can Assist Sales Effort

Salespeople often complain that restrictive company credit policies put a damper on their sales volume by limiting the number of potential customers. Yet the real problem is that salespeople often waste valuable selling time on customers who, because of financial weakness, will never deliver profitable volume.

The credit department can help the sales force in the following ways:

Show Salespeople Where to Concentrate their Effort

The credit unit can provide people in the field with lists of accounts in their territories whose credit is good beyond current volume. Salespeople should be trying to expand the business they do with those accounts.

The credit staff can also guide them on accounts to avoid by providing weekly or monthly lists of past-due accounts, as well as lists of those whose credit limits have been reached for the present. At the same time, salespeople should be informed without delay when overdue accounts are paid up and therefore can be contacted for more orders.

Enlist Sales People's Help in Establishing the Creditworthiness of Accounts

Salespeople usually start calling on an account long before an order is finally taken. Each week, credit personnel should receive from salespeople a list of potential new accounts so that preliminary checking can be completed. This cuts down on the time it takes to process initial orders and allows the credit department to alert salespeople to potential problems with credit and sales terms.

Observation

Salespeople should understand their interest in sound credit practices. On a profit margin of, say, 5 percent, a loss of $100 due to poor credit would take $2,000 in added sales to recoup. Salespeople can help avoid credit problems by treating payment policies as part of the selling job.

Encourage the Credit Department's Active Participation in Sales

Joint visits to key accounts by the credit executive and salespeople can improve goodwill while enabling the credit manager to better evaluate credit risk. The credit manager may suggest financing arrangements to facilitate a sale. The counsel of the credit manager might even be offered to certain customers, regarding ways to improve their collection practices to achieve better cash flow and thus increase their buying power.

6 Managing Collections to Maximize Cash Flow

There are two sides to all effective credit management programs. The first, of course, is deciding who gets credit and how much to grant. If this task is performed wisely, the second–managing your accounts receivable–should not become too much of a burden.

Examine Your Accounts Receivable Policies

Regardless of whether your company is feeling the pinch of outstanding receivables at present, chances are that you could benefit from a top-level review of credit practices.

All customers can be expected to try to live on their suppliers' capital. Indeed, stretching out payments is becoming an accepted way of doing business. But unpaid bills are, in effect, interest-free loans to customers. Few suppliers can afford to extend this privilege indefinitely. Even minor stretchouts of payments can add up to a costly burden. What is more, tightening receivables policies may be your best way to unlock capital for more profitable uses. Yet competitive factors complicate the picture.

As business costs continue to rise and the competition becomes increasingly keen, credit terms take on a more important role in clinching sales. In many industries, credit has become as important to winning business-to-business sales as it has proved to be in winning consumer sales. Where does your company stand in the receivables picture? Even more important, where will it stand in the months to come?

As the first step in appraising collectibility, conduct a process that's called aging the accounts receivable. To do this, total the accounts receivable outstanding at the end of the most recent month. Then break the total down into percent current, past-due 30 days, 60 days, 90 days and so forth.

At this point, look at the larger delinquencies. Why have not the accounts been paid? Was the credit justified in the first place? Have the proper collection efforts been made? What's the potential loss, if any?

If you provide special dating or credit terms, take a look at the number of such transactions currently in force, and the amounts, compared with past years. Satisfy yourself that they were justified by special circumstances and are not overextensions of credit.

Recommendation

To gain insight into present credit authorization procedures, review the investigations behind some recent authorizations—both for new accounts and for boosts in credit limits for established customers. Look into the credit folders on some older accounts. How recently have the financial data and payment records been updated?

This kind of analysis can take some time. But if a preliminary test leaves any doubt in your mind, a more extensive review will justify the effort.

Is your reserve for bad-debt losses adequate? In light of your spot-checks, above, and your own loss experience, how does your reserve stack up? Does the amount tied up in 90-day-old (or older) receivables exceed your present reserve by as much as 2:1?

If so, it does not necessarily mean that actual losses will be proportionate. But it does mean that you are facing some tough collection problems that could lead to this result unless you take aggressive steps promptly. Take special note of any large overdue balances from marginal risks, the kind that would be the first to be in trouble if sales fell off.

- Are collection practices consistent with today's climate? Are overdue amounts immediately brought to the attention of the individual responsible for follow-up? Do the files show a pattern of prompt and continuous efforts to collect? Are collections being hampered by disputes with customers? Is there an unwritten agreement between the credit and sales departments to take it easy because of competition?

- Would your company be embarrassed if there were any further significant slowing in collections? If you regularly project cash flow, a glance will tell you how important receivables collections are to any scheduled expenditures, even in paying your regular bills. Compare your cash versus trade payables plus any unusual expenditures (machine purchase, loan repayment and so forth) coming up. Would it be necessary (and possible) to go to your banker if a large account suddenly did not pay up?

- If your spot-checks raise strong doubts about your receivables position, you may want to consider an account-by-account examination against updated credit files. Sometimes called the cold turkey method, it is used in cases of bulk sales or when receivables have been pledged as security. Such an examination provides clear insight into the worth of outstanding accounts, especially in the event of a sharp business downturn.

Observation

You may be reluctant to dig into an apparently smooth-running operation for fear of creating a confidence crisis. But such probing may reveal that the apparent smoothness was deceptive. Experience has often shown that what may appear as tiny cracks on the credit surface may turn out, on closer examination, to be dangerous crevasses.

Clearly, no company wants to risk tightening its credit policy in an industry where the competition is going the other way—offering open accounts, say, or other special deals. But do not lose sight of the fact that top-heavy receivables are a costly burden, even in a growth economy.

Check Performance with Variance Analysis

The average collection period expresses, in days, the average time it takes to collect bills for any given month. A rising average collection period can lead to serious problems and should trigger a vigorous effort to speed up collections.

Three steps are involved in calculating an average collection period for your company:

1. Find the percentage of sales collected for a given month in 0-30 days, 30-60 days, 60-90 days and 90+ days.
2. Multiply the percentage for each aging category by its midpoint in days (15 days for the 0-30 category; 45 for the 30-60; 75 for the 60-90; and 105 for the 90+).

Illustration

You determine that your December sales were collected in the following manner: 4 percent in 0–30 days, 50 percent in 30–60 days, 45 percent in 60–90 days and 1 percent in 90+ days. Here is how your calculations would look:

15 days x .04 = 0.60
45 days x .50 = 22.50
75 days x .45 = 33.75
105 days x .01 = 1.05
57.90 = 58 days

Your average collection period for that particular month's receivables is 58 days.

3. Add the average days in each category to arrive at the average collection period.

Improving Your Collection Process

In most cases, collection efforts begin as an account matures and extend for a maximum of 90 days. By then the account either has been paid up or has been presented for collection. A schedule for collection efforts appears on page 97. There are three definite phases to the collection process. Each has its own particular set of operating procedures:

Collection Phase 1 (1–30 Days Overdue)

Although the first phase of the collection effort officially begins on the day after an account matures, few firms start to take action that early. Allowing for mail delays and an official grace period, collection proceedings usually begin somewhere between the 35th and 40th day after the invoice date, rather than on day 31, the first day overdue. By that time, most payments will have been received.

Invoice Copies

A handy collection tool. For many collection managers, a rubber stamp and invoice copy are the most valuable tools in the entire collection process. When an invoice is issued, a copy is sent to the collection department and filed in a tickler file, coinciding with the day it matures.

Then, as the first step in the collection process, a copy of the invoice is pulled, stamped past due and sent to the customer. This can take the place of the first collection letter (see collection schedule above). What is more, it has proved to be an effective attention getter.

Observation

One month's average has little significance. You will need to compare the average with previous months and your year-ago figures. A 1-month aberration may not be serious, but a 3-month upswing could spell trouble.

Monthly Statements

Use a stamp and an invoice. If your firm sends out monthly statements, you can modify the above procedure by attaching a copy of the past due invoice to the statement. The stamped invoice calls attention to your statement and takes the place of the first letter. Moreover, attaching an invoice copy can speed payments from companies that find it difficult to locate past-due items on the skimpy evidence provided by a monthly statement.

In subsequent monthly statements, you should add a short note requesting payment. Merely point out which items are past due or, if a letter was written, refer to it.

Suggested Schedule for Collection Procedures	
5 days overdue	Send invoice stamped Past Due.
15 days overdue	Send first letter requesting immediate payment.
30 days overdue	Send second letter demanding immediate payment.
40 days overdue	Follow up letter with phone call–or make personal visit to customer–to find out why payment is late. Agree on a time when a payment will be made, or negotiate installments.
45 days overdue	If the above steps have not worked, send third letter demanding payment on a seriously delinquent account.
55 days overdue	Follow up letter with phone call stating that customer's payment must be made by a certain date. Emphasize serious consequences of further delay. If necessary, offer alternative payment terms.
60 days overdue	Continue efforts to work with customer to settle acount.
75 days overdue	If all efforts have failed, write a fourth and final letter informing customer that you will take action to collect by a specific date.
90 days overdue	Follow through on action described in the letter.

Collection Letters

Form letters, once the mainstay of most collection efforts, have been replaced by computer-generated letters. Collection letters are usually used every 10-15 days, with the tone of the letters becoming progressively tougher throughout the cycle.

> **Observation**
>
> If the same customer has an order pending, you might write a statement note saying, Payment will enable us to ship order #7650.

A properly drawn series of collection letters can significantly lower your outstanding receivables. Moreover, since a company now can mix and match paragraphs on a computer, collection letters have become easier to craft. A well-written collection letter is an effective means of handling large numbers of accounts with relatively small past-due items. (See the sample letters on pages 99-102)

Observation

Collection letters have many uses but one large drawback: They are seldom effective in dealing with serious collection problems. Most collection letter series include only four letters to be sent at 10- to 15-day intervals. The four-letter series is used because past experience has shown that a collection letter seldom has any impact on a customer whose bills are already 2 months overdue. That type of customer takes special handling, as we shall see later.

Collection Phase 2 (30–60 Days Overdue)

The second phase of the collection process is the most critical. When a customer does not respond to early collection efforts, you may be sure that you and the customer have a serious problem. Here, the skill of collection personnel comes into play. They must find out what the problem is and attempt to resolve it without alienating the customer and possibly losing the account's business.

Because the problem is rapidly approaching the crisis stage in the second phase, you should intensify your efforts. Continue to leave 10 to 15 days between follow-up efforts to avoid the appearance of harassment. However, in addition to the normal collection letter series, also consider a personal letter or a phone call. Even a personal visit may be warranted if the situation is serious enough. In addition, your collector should use his negotiating skills to secure at least partial payment in as short a time as possible.

You can tailor the message portion of the collection letter to address the specific problem you're having with your client. This sort of collection letter has met with a great deal of success, particularly when used in conjunction with a personal visit or telephone call. Also, always use the telephone for high-risk accounts and customers who have sizable past-due bills.

Recommendation

Negotiating with your customers can be a difficult task. Naturally, you value their business and do not wish to jeopardize your relationship. At the same time, however, you cannot afford to allow overdue bills to go unpaid.

Sample Collection Letter 1
(5–15 Days Overdue)

Nuts & Bolts Company, Inc.
Supplier Drive
Smithville, Anystate

[date]

I.M.N. Entrepreneur President
Widgets Unlimited
Manufacturing Drive
Anytown, Anystate 00000

Dear Mr. Entrepreneur:

According to our records, payment for your order of [for services performed on] ________ is overdue. Enclosed is a copy of our invoice #________ in the amount of $ ________ for this order [these services].

If you have already sent your payment, thank you. If not, please forward it promptly so we can bring your account up-to-date.

Yours truly,

J.J. Smith
Credit Manager

Sample Collection Letter 2
(30 Days Overdue)

Nuts & Bolts Company, Inc.
Supplier Drive
Smithville, Anystate 00000

[date]

I.M.N. Entrepreneur
President Widgets
Unlimited Manufacturing Drive
Anytown, Anystate 00000

Dear Mr. Entrepreneur:

We wrote you on ________ to alert you to the fact that the payment for your order of [for services performed on] ________ is overdue. But we have not received your check since then.

Please send your payment in the amount of $ ________ immediately. We'd like to bring your account up-to-date and ship your current order.

If your check is already in the mail, thank you.

Yours truly,

J.J. Smith
Credit Manager

Sample Collection Letter 3
(45 Days Overdue)

Nuts & Bolts Company, Inc.
Supplier Drive
Smithville, Anystate

[date]

I.M.N. Entrepreneur President
Widgets Unlimited
Manufacturing Drive
Anytown, Anystate 00000

Dear Mr. Entrepreneur:

This is our third letter requesting payment for your order of [for services performed on] ________. Your account is seriously delinquent, and we still have not received your check.

Late payments cost our company money and affect your company's credit rating. Please send your payment in the amount of $ ________ immediately. We'd like to continue to do business with your firm.

Yours truly,

J.J. Smith
Credit Manager

Sample Collection Letter 4 (60 or More Days Overdue)

Nuts & Bolts Company, Inc.
Supplier Drive
Smithville, Anystate

[date]

I.M.N. Entrepreneur President
Widgets Unlimited
Manufacturing Drive
Anytown, Anystate 00000

Dear Mr. Entrepreneur:

This is our fourth and final letter about the overdue payment for your order of [for services performed on] ________. We have tried to contact you by phone several times during the past month but have been unable to reach you.

Please send your payment in the amount of $ ________ at once to preserve your company's good credit rating. Otherwise, you'll leave us with no choice but to turn your delinquent account over to an outside agency for collection.

We look forward to receiving your check in the next few days.

Yours truly,

J.J. Smith
Credit Manager

Unpaid Ad Infinitum

Call a customer's bank on all agreements for large bills. You will want to know that the customer is financially able to keep a promise to pay. When you know that a negotiating session is approaching, it might be a good idea to do this beforehand.

Final Collection Phase (60 or More Days Overdue)

There is no precise beginning or end to the final collection phase. It starts when it becomes apparent that all normal collection procedures have failed. It ends when a settlement has been made or you drop your effort. As with all collection methods, the final stage is an attempt to communicate the urgency of your message.

If, by the 60th day, the customer still has not given you any indication that payment will be made, send a letter with an attorney's signature and also phone the account. The attorney need not be a collection specialist. What you are after in this instance is the attorney's clout.

"Arrange with your corporate counsel to use his name and address in your letter," advises collection expert A. Michael Coleman. "Ask for this as an accommodation if you are paying your counsel on a retainer basis, in exchange for any accounts that ultimately do require legal intervention. Never pay the attorney a percentage of collections from the letter but, if necessary, offer an additional $500 to $1,000 a year as an inducement."

Keep in mind that a demand letter from an attorney often carries as much weight with a customer as the threat of a lawsuit. As a result, such a letter is normally quite effective in stimulating payment action.

Recommendation

State that all calls be directed to your company or collection agency. Do not put the attorney's phone number in the letter.

If you reach the 75th day past due and (a) your customer is local and (b) nonpayment is due to a disagreement over payment, delivery terms or product quality, suggest taking the dispute to your area's Better Business Bureau for arbitration. Be aware, however, that if you and your customer agree to abide by the arbitrator's decision, it will be legally binding. Better Business Bureaus are not-for-profit organizations and do not charge a fee for arbitration.

If any of these options do not work in your case, send your fourth and final letter to the customer. Tell the company you will turn the account over to a collection attorney or agency if you do not receive payment by a certain date. Then, if the payment does not arrive by the specified day, follow through by placing the account with the attorney or agency. You have exhausted all other possibilities.

If the Debt Is $500 or Less

If the debt is small, turning it over for collection will probably not be worthwhile financially. Instead, make one final call to try to persuade the debtor to pay you.

A worthwhile tactic, says Coleman, is the withdrawal technique. Briefly, you give the debtor the impression that you are giving up by admitting that you have no intention of suing because it would not be worthwhile. But instead of just saying goodbye, ask the debtor how important it is for his firm to continue doing business on credit for the next 7 years. Then proceed to explain that you will report the unpaid debt to credit-reporting bureaus, including the trade associations in the account's industry. Tell the customer that his bad-debt report will stay on the record for 7 years.

Is it really worth it for the sake of $380, you might ask, to have a major credit decision go against your firm because the decision maker assumes you are not a good credit risk? If the debtor decides the answer is no, says Coleman, you win.

Observation

Most companies prefer to use an attorney to collect overdue accounts simply because an attorney does not carry the stigma of a collection agency. Also, an attorney often can collect the overdue bill while preserving the account as well. Your present counsel may not want to take on the specialized task of acting as a collection attorney. If so, he can probably recommend an experienced collection attorney in your area. However, be prepared for rather high fees. They can run $125 per hour or more, up to as much as one-third of the debt.

If the Debt Is More Than $500

You could take your delinquent customer to small-claims court if the amount in dispute is under a certain cutoff–usually a few thousand dollars, depending on state maximums. Be sure you have the evidence ready to support your claim and that you have a reasonable chance of collecting (see page 106). Note, too, that even if both of those factors are in your favor, you may be better off trying to collect through an attorney or a collection agency.

Selecting the Right Collection Agency

If you prefer using a collection agency, shop around for a reputable firm that offers reliable service at an equitable fee. You can opt for a nationwide service, such as that offered by Dun & Bradstreet, or a local or regional agency in your area. If you choose the latter, be sure the agency has a representative in your customer's area.

The National Association of Credit Management, with its nationwide network of local credit and collection agencies in 53 cities, can give you a referral. To locate the branch nearest you, contact the NACM at (410) 740-5560 or visit *www.nacm.org*.

Do Not Take Anything for Granted

Check out the references and reputation of the collection agency carefully. Also ask to see the collector's certificate of bonding. Walk away from any agency that is hesitant.

As you check the collector's references, try to ascertain that you will receive all the services you will pay for. Specifically, ask the agency's clients questions such as:

- How promptly does the agency remit collected balances to clients? If it takes more than a day or two, think about looking elsewhere.
- How often does the agency review its progress with you? Monthly reports are the least you should expect, with news of significant developments passed along as they occur.

Find a Collector that Knows Your Business

If at all possible, use a collection agency that is familiar with your industry. You stand to benefit from such a relationship in two ways. First, it will help to have an agency that is familiar with your industry's payment practices. Second, if your collector has built up a reputation for efficiency within your industry, it could convince customers to speed payments.

Caution

When checking out the collector's reputation, keep in mind that laws covering unsavory collection techniques have been toughened in recent years. Because the collector is your agent, you are liable for its actions if it should cross over the line into harassment. Your Better Business Bureau or your local chapter of the National Association of Credit Management can give you guidance on the firm's past record.

Make Sure Fees Are Competitive

Collection fees are based on the amounts collected. Rates can vary from 20 percent to 40 percent, so look around if your agency's rates are appreciably higher. Note: On small amounts ($100 to $200) the percentage rate can go as high as 50 percent, and most collection agencies do not want to handle them.

Recommendation

When you finally choose a collection agency, do not make its job tough by waiting too long to submit accounts. You will find that your agency can do a better job for you if you turn over accounts to it in 60–90 days instead of waiting 120 days or longer.

If You Decide to Sue

First, be sure that you have exhausted all other avenues of redress. It is costly to sue, and if you lose, you may end up having to eat legal and court costs as well as the debt.

Next, be sure that you have a chance of collecting if you win. If the account has federal tax liens or other unpaid creditor judgments outstanding against it, you have little chance of being paid even if you win your case. So always search the public records–for pending litigation, judgments and tax liens–before you file a suit.

"There are reputable search firms that can retrieve this information for you at minimal cost," Coleman says. One is CSC (Corporation Service Co.) in Richmond, Va.; phone (800) 872-4636.

Observation

To force a debtor into involuntary bankruptcy, you usually need a minimum of three petitioners whose unsecured claims total at least $5,000. Consult with your attorney if you are considering this or any of the other avenues mentioned above.

"Court records can also be helpful," he adds. "They will not only tell you whether your account has judgments outstanding against it, but also whether it is currently in litigation. If you find other creditors are suing, you may be able to join forces. Together you might be able to force the account into involuntary bankruptcy, initiate equitable remedies or develop criteria for a summary judgment or property attachment."

7
Streamlining Collection Procedures

Slow customer payments can reduce a smaller company's available cash faster than almost any other financial problem. To keep your accounts receivable from running away with your company's cash flow, try streamlining your billing and collection procedures. In this section we discuss several practical ideas that will improve your collections.

Simplify Your Invoices

Design an invoice that's easy to read. Avoid the clutter of too much print so that the important data–amount due, due date and any overdue amounts–stand out.

Enclose a stamped, self-addressed envelope, or a window envelope and return-address invoice, so that your customer's bookkeeper will need only to write a check, stuff the envelope and put it in the mail.

Alert customers to overdue accounts by color-coding overdue bills and/or by including a section on the bill highlighting payments that are 30, 60 or 90 days overdue. (At this point you will already have contacted the customer by phone or letter about the delinquent account.)

Give Customers an Incentive to Pay Early

The traditional 2 percent discount for payments made within 10 days of delivery has lost most of its value as an incentive for early payment of bills. Even when interest rates are only moderately high, most customers prefer to forgo the discount and pay their bills at or near the end of the usual 30-day net period. Worse, others pay in 30 days and take the discount anyway. These practices can add significantly to the cost of maintaining your accounts receivable.

By replacing the 2/10-net 30 standard discount with one based on just how early payment is made, you encourage faster payment and discourage cheating. Under this system, a simple formula links the discount rate to the payment date. Thus, a payment received 15 days before the net due date (usually 30 days after delivery) would receive a larger discount than one received 10 days early.

Observation

Such a system not only provides your customers with an added inducement to settle their accounts quickly but also smooths out the flow of your incoming payments rather than having them bunched up at the due date.

Obviously, a realistic discount rate is central to success. It must be high enough to provide your customers with sufficient incentive to forward their checks before the due date, but low enough to keep your cash flow at the proper level.

Users of such a system generally employ a formula based on their internal cost of capital. Keep in mind that this refers not only to what it costs them to borrow money but also to the real average cost of all capital invested in the firm, including equity. Granting a discount equivalent to the firm's cost of capital rate maintains cash flow while still offering customers an attractive premium over other investment rates.

Once you decide on an appropriate discount rate, the calculation is simple:

Discount = cost of capital ÷ 365 x days early x balance due

Obtain Information on Problem Accounts

In addition to placing a financial burden on small and midsize firms, overdue accounts can cause administrative headaches. Without a credit manager to keep tabs on problem customers, the task usually falls by default to senior management, which can ill afford to take time away from duties more directly associated with sales and profit improvement.

Illustration

A customer pays an invoice (amounting to $2,600) 11 days before the due date. If your cost of capital worked out to 20 percent, your discount calculation would be as follows:

Discount = .20 ÷ 365 x 11 x $2,600 = $15.67

In other words, your customer would receive a credit of $15.67 for settling his account 11 days early. If the check had arrived 20 days early, the credit would have amounted to $28.50.

As an alternative, you could employ outside services to acquire as much information as you need regarding developments at problem customers. Two such services, available from Dun & Bradstreet Receivable Management Services, are particularly appropriate for small and midsize firms that cannot justify a full-blown credit department.

Observation

A penalty charge for late payments can be calculated in similar fashion. If the amount in the above example arrived 11 days late, the late charge would be $15.67.

A Quick Check on Your Delinquent Accounts

The first service is called Debt-Scan. It involves a one-time check on your customer to determine D&B's collection experience over the previous 12 months. The Scan report will list any claims by other creditors, note whether they have been settled and, if they have, on what terms.

Thus, if you find that a delinquent customer already has two or three claims placed for collection, you might want to file your own claim immediately. If the record is clean, it might indicate that your situation is an isolated one, which could be worked out without a collection agency's involvement.

Observation

A clean record with D&B does not guarantee that the company being investigated has no collection problems because it only mirrors D&B's experience with the company. However, since D&B Receivable Management Services is one of the largest commercial collection agencies in the country and keeps data on close to two million third-party letter demand and collection experiences, it is unlikely that a company could be in serious difficulty without D&B knowing about it.

A Way to Monitor Developments at Problem Accounts

The second type of creditor service offered by Dun & Bradstreet is called Debt-Alert. This takes the Debt-Scan concept one step further. Subscribers receive monthly reports on all problem accounts that are registered with D&B, including information on claim settlements, payment data and any other changes in the status of the problem account. In other words, Debt-Alert provides you with the information necessary to make informed decisions on how best to proceed with accounts seriously in arrears.

Prices for the two services vary with the number of accounts registered. However, as a guideline, you can submit up to 100 accounts for Debt-Scan over a 12-month period for a $435 fee. Fees for Debt-Alert are tailored to your company's individual needs but usually range somewhere between $500 and $1,500 per year for a midsize firm.

For further information, contact your local D&B sales office or Dun & Bradstreet Receivable Management Services at One Diamond Hill Road, Murray Hill, NJ 07974; phone (800) 333-6497. Or visit its Website: *www.smallbusiness.dnb.com/collect-debt/duns-demand-series-detail.asp*, where you'll find many other product offerings, such as outsourcing, letter-writing programs and its Recovery Score system, which allows D&B to determine how likely a particular customer is to pay your overdue bills.

Improve Collection Letters to Speed Payments

Many consumer and industrial companies are revamping credit practices to reduce the number of overdue accounts. However, the very wording of letters sent to delinquent customers is often overlooked because it is usually taken for granted. Revisions in copy and approach may prove to be a relatively simple way to improve cash flow and, in the final analysis, accomplish more than a personal phone call or the other, more subtle techniques. For instance:

Keep Letters Short and Concise

They should be easy to read and leave no doubt as to your message. Letters that sound personal tend to work better than those that are clearly form letters. Using your computer, they are almost as easy to turn out. A P.S. can be an effective attention-getter, so use it to present your strongest points briefly.

Look for these common mistakes in reviewing collection letters:

- **Negative tone**
  Surprise, disappointment, irritation and impatience all are natural responses to delinquent accounts but are inappropriate in a letter. Equally ineffective is an apologetic tone. The tone of the letter, in the early stages of the collection program, should be thoroughly fact-oriented: The customer promised to pay by a certain date, so please pay.
- **Built-in excuse**
  If there is any problem with your order, please let us know is a frequent but needless phrase found in collection letters. Instead, the letter should reflect the confident assumption that payment will be made. And it should not cite reasons why payment might be late. If early reminders have been fruitless, the next step is to ask for either payment or an explanation immediately, and offer considerate treatment if the customer wishes to talk about the bill.
- **Backtracking**
  Each letter in a collection series should be increasingly forceful. Thus it is a mistake, after several notices have been sent to a customer, to start asking if there was an oversight. This only encourages a let 'em wait reaction. After two or three reminders, it is time to develop an urgent tone implying that there is little time left to resolve the matter before action is taken.
- **Threats**
  It is illegal to threaten to sue unless you follow through. In fact, any toothless threats are a bad idea. "Ultimatums tend to prompt the debtor to do just the opposite of what you demand," collection consultant A. Michael Coleman notes. The best approach, unless the bill is long overdue, is to sell the benefits of prompt payment while keeping threats understated. An example of positive wording from an effective collection letter used by one hardware manufacturer:

> With your reputation for prompt payment, we are glad to have you as a customer. Although your payment is now 30 days past due, you can keep your credit standing by sending payment immediately.

The series of collection letters should establish a picture of a firm that is–above all–businesslike but also understanding, ever-patient under mitigating circumstances and, finally, no patsy.

Use Salesmanship to Improve Your Results

Keep in mind that recipients of collection letters pay more attention to letters that involve their point of view. For example: We have always appreciated the way you have consistently kept your account and your credit standing up-to-date. That is why we are concerned . . .

Direct salesmanship is not out of place. For instance, you might want to add, The next time you are in town, please stop by and look over our new showroom. This implies that you are confident payment will be made and that you want to continue your relationship with the customer.

Try to Keep the Reader Sold on Your Company.

Whether you are turning down a customer's request for additional credit or a request for information you cannot divulge, before stating your refusal, justify your reason from the reader's point of view. Throughout the letter, retain an attitude of helpfulness. Where called for, end with a counterproposal that may be acceptable to the reader.

Here is a condensed example showing how these principles might be applied to a letter turning down a request for more credit:

> Your December order for $22,000 indicates that you are selling a lot of our components. We find this most gratifying.
>
> To help you keep up with demand, we need to know whether this order means you have outgrown the credit arrangements you made with us 2 years ago. This shipment would put you some $4,000 beyond credit limits we had agreed on. The information you sent us, however, indicates that you may be overstocking our products.
>
> If, after reviewing your needs, you still want $22,000 of our product now, you can stock the extra $4,000 worth of this popular line by paying cash and taking advantage of the 2 percent discount for at least part of your order. Or you might reduce the size of your order . . .

Pros and Cons of Using Collection Letter Services

If you does not been approached by a collection letter-writing service, you soon may be. They offer to send a series of collection letters (usually four) to your overdue accounts in return for an upfront fee from you.

The fee usually ranges from $5 to $8 per account, and most agencies claim a collection rate in the 50 percent to 60 percent range. Even though this may sound attractive, consider the following before you sign a contract:

What Are Your Own Capabilities?

If you have the equipment and personnel to follow up on late payers and delinquent

Recommendation

In the interest of directness and clarity, business letters should be free of outmoded, deadwood phrases. Check your correspondence for phrases such as Permit me to take this opportunity. . .instead of simply Thank you for. . .; We are in receipt of. . .instead of The problem you refer to in your letter probably stems from. . .or In accordance with your request. . .Instead of We will be glad to. . .

Observation

In recent years, there has been an increasing trend toward less formality in business correspondence, due at least in part to cost concerns. For example, window envelopes, along with smaller stationery, are often used for acknowledgments, answering inquiries and other purposes, not just for bills or promotional letters.

accounts with your own series of letters, you do not need an outside service to do the job for you.

How Serious are Your Collection Problems?

Collection letter services are most effective when used to secure payment from overdue accounts that are bothersome but have not yet become deep-seated problems. If you use a collection letter service for all your late accounts, you may wind up paying as much as $8 for a single letter. You would have been better off writing that one letter yourself. Collection letter services are also likely to be ineffective against a customer who is unwilling or unable to pay.

Will You Need Additional Collection Help?

If you use a letter-writing service, you probably will need backup from a full-service collection agency to handle your thorniest accounts. Some letter services are associated with a collection service; some are not. Find out beforehand whether the service meets your needs. What's more, be sure that the collection agency measures up. (See pages 105-106.)

> **Caution**
>
> In your dealings with a collection letter-writing service, keep in mind that an upfront fee carries with it the potential for abuse. Watch out for any contract that may require payment for letters you never use.

Making Collection Calls More Effective

Like telephone sales calls, telephone collection efforts must be carefully planned and professionally handled. If you do them in-house, train your people to catch the past-due account's interest by referring to the account's reputation and expressing both your company's interest in resolving the problem and your assumption that the firm has every intention of paying you.

Instead of using a phrase such as–After you have paid,–which collection expert Coleman says has a negative connotation, use–After this matter is resolved or When we have received your check. Both are positive and imply that the account will pay. Some other tips from Coleman:

- **Pace your delivery**
  If the person at the past-due account speaks slowly, match his pace. If he speaks very rapidly, keep your pace slower to encourage a slower, calmer and more rational response from him. Also, match the person's conversational style in terms of sophistication.

- **Watch your posture**
  It affects your voice. When you slump, your voice also slumps. You may even find it helpful to stand or walk around while talking.
- Show you are listening
  Respond to the other party's statements with comments such as, Yes, and I see.

Handling Returned Checks

Inevitably, your collection department will be faced with the problem of what to do with a bounced check. Checks can be returned for a variety of reasons, not all of which are the fault of your customer. In every case, however, you should act quickly and follow up closely. Here are some of the principal reasons for returned checks and how to handle them:

- **Insufficient funds**
  Redeposit the check if it comes from a good customer. Then call the customer, mentioning what you have done, and ask that the customer check his bank to make sure that the check clears. If a check from a marginal customer is returned marked insufficient funds, call immediately and ask for a certified check by return mail. Hold the returned check until the new one is received.
- **Account closed**
  Sometimes you can get caught in the turmoil that can follow when a customer changes banks. Call. If that is what happened, the customer is likely to send a new check immediately. However, the customer may have moved or gone out of business. If you cannot reach your customer, place the account with a collection agency.
- **Uncollected funds**
  This is the easiest type of returned check to handle. Usually, if the check is redeposited, it will clear. To be on the safe side, however, call your customer and let him know what has happened to the check.

When the Customer Is Nearly Bankrupt

It will not help to drive the company closer to the edge. Instead, offer the company a very lean payment plan–one the firm can afford–with the understanding that payments will increase later. If even this is impossible, your alternatives are dwindling. If the customer is worthy or the account balance is hefty, consider a new tactic: Offer the company help in restructuring its finances, working with other creditors through a formal extension agreement.

Under the terms of such agreements, participating creditors defer collection if the debtor (your customer) agrees to certain conditions and accepts specific obligations. A creditors committee is elected at a meeting of general creditors (usually held under the aegis of a trade association, such as the National Association of Credit Management). This committee monitors the debtor's financial operations and planning and advises the company about major decisions that have a bearing on its financial recovery. If, after a period of time, repayment seems unlikely, the committee will terminate the agreement or take some other action.

If you and your customer's other creditors decide to join forces in an extension agreement, be sure that most of the participants agree on the plan. Otherwise, it will not get off the ground. And make certain that your customer's secured creditors will cooperate with you; they have the first claim in collecting overdue payments. From your viewpoint, an extension agreement certainly beats the debt reorganization that follows a bankruptcy filing, when you and the other creditors divvy up the leavings of a disaster.

From your customer's standpoint, the agreement is less likely to result in liquidation of the company's assets than a Chapter 11. It also avoids the stigma of bankruptcy. Since creditors participating in an extension agreement usually waive interest on the customer's payments, the procedure probably costs a debtor no more than filing a Chapter 11.

8 Unsound Practices—Recommended Cures

The most practical solution for a business with credit and collection problems is to re-examine its current practices for unsound elements and then weed them out. Checklisted below are the weaknesses most commonly uncovered in an audit of credit practices. Each is followed by a series of recommendations for corrective action.

In most companies, one or more of these unsound practices will show up; only the degree of sensitivity will vary. While some of the deficiencies–and some of the suggestions–may seem too basic to apply to your company, it would be very unusual if none of them applied in any degree.

Unsound Practice No. 1

Inefficient Credit Operations . . . due to lack of proper training and/or inadequate supervision (found primarily in small and rapidly growing firms):

This is evident where credit functions–such as investigation, establishment of credit lines and collection follow-up–are largely unsupervised. Instead, they are left to the discretion of lower-echelon credit or accounting personnel, who work without established procedures and virtually without systematic supervision. As a result, practices such as the following tend to develop:

- Superficial credit investigation, such as assigning substantial lines of credit to new, borderline accounts solely on a book rating or agency report, without requiring up-to-date credit data directly from the customer.
- Overextension to marginal risks. Haphazard collection efforts, unsystematic collection follow-up and foggy understanding of progressive collection appeals.
- Indefinite or excessive time extended to unresponsive delinquents.
- A lenient attitude toward customers who, having extra terms, still fail to pay on time.
- Marginal credit risks carried considerably beyond the due date without shutting off credit and applying pressure.

The Cure

Where some variation of this problem exists, a company may take two basic steps:

1. Inaugurate (or update) a credit and collection policy manual detailing policies, procedures and methods. It should include:
   - Ground rules for investigation of new accounts and periodic updating of existing credit files. Guidelines should explain in detail what data are required and where to get the information.
   - Instructions on how to evaluate credit data and establish credit lines.
   - Standard collection procedures, including starting schedule, intervals between collection follow-up and general methods.
   - Explanation of motivations behind the progressive collection appeals you use.
   - Limitations on time to be extended to unresponsive delinquents.
   - Philosophy of credit and its uses.
   - Other requisites peculiar to the individual business.

   Although such a policy may seem elementary in some respects, it nevertheless has a valuable purpose. It serves as a foundation for day-to-day credit decision making, a directive for establishing requirements and a means of facilitating orderly and systematic procedures.

Smaller firms lacking a credit manager and staff need such basic guidelines at least as much as a larger company with a full-fledged credit department does. An excellent source of guidance is the *Credit Professional's Handbook*, prepared by the Credit Research Foundation, 8815 Centre Park Drive, Columbia, MD 21045. This reference volume includes coverage of credit policy design and implementation; credit department administration and reporting systems; techniques for evaluating accounts-receivable portfolios, collection procedures and automated credit and accounts-receivable systems; and a discussion of international credit. For further information, contact CRF at (410) 740-5499 or visit its Website at *www.crfonline.org*.

2. Establish mandatory periods for review of credit activities, down to and including perusal of credit files and follow-up files.

   Such reviews should be scheduled at 30- to 60-day intervals, depending on factors such as the experience and capabilities of your credit staff and the typical amount of credit extended per customer.

   Comments and suggestions resulting from the review should be confirmed in writing and subsequently followed through. This is just an application of the oldest rule of management: Be sure that requirements are clearly understood; then see to it that instructions are carried out.

   You can make it clear to your credit people that systematic review or supervision is not necessarily a reflection on anyone's competence. Rather, it serves the purpose of insurance on a major asset; it provides a fundamental safeguard over a high-risk responsibility.

Unsound Practice No. 2

Growing Permissiveness . . . with customers taking advantage of competitive practices to break down your firm's credit standards:

Where this weakness exists, you will find numerous instances of yielding to unreasonable demands for open account terms. Customers will also tend to help themselves to unauthorized concessions, such as unearned cash discounts and extra time in settling accounts.

While it may be expected that some latitude will be applied in highly profitable or competitive situations, the practice of permitting any account to take such liberties can only lead from liberal credit to credit license.With weak credit risks, permitting self-serving concessions is asking for double trouble; sooner or later, it will be necessary to face up to the problem.

The Cure

Strong reforms can correct this situation:

1. Do not accept at face value claims about what the competition is doing.
2. Bear in mind that it is a rare case where credit terms are the deciding factor in a decision to purchase one product or another. More often, the open account is merely thrown in to sweeten the deal.

   You cannot contact your competitors, of course, to find out what they are doing, but you can ask for more evidence (from your salespeople, for example) than the buyer's unsupported statement. In fact, you could be in trouble if you do not; discrimination in credit terms can be a violation of the Robinson-Patman Act. Try to secure payment from financially weak customers through one of the many credit devices available, such as letters of credit or personal guarantees. (See page 85.)
3. Make some effort to get financially able accounts to pay promptly.

   Do not hesitate to contact them individually or send out a carefully worded reminder letter. Over the years, some companies have won results with a light touch or a subtle prodding.

   Other firms are getting results by discussing the problem frankly with such customers. Obviously, it must be done in ways that avoid implying that you–or they–are on shaky ground. One technique is to have a general executive make the approach rather than a credit or financial person so that the matter can be discussed on an easy, executive-to-executive basis.
4. See that collections from marginal accounts are handled with firmness appropriate to the quality of such risks.
5. The classic be flexible, be firm concept should be applied, with due emphasis on the latter point when needed. Since marginal risks account for a high proportion of collection problems, there would seem to be little reason to be lenient after payment performance has confirmed your initial premise.

6. Handle delinquencies on special-terms billing differently from those on regular-terms billing. It may be sound practice to allow some latitude on past-due invoices carrying regular terms, but a line has to be drawn on special-terms billing. It should be presumed that customers with the latter forfeit the right to any further breathing spell when extra terms are granted at the outset.

   Applying extraordinary lenience is, in effect, nurturing a problem account. It is far better in the long run to take firm steps at the first sign of potential difficulty.

7. Solve the tricky problem of customers taking unearned cash discounts. There are customers who pay late enough to lose the privilege of a discount for speedy payment but take it anyway. You have most of the payment, but how do you get the rest and avoid a repetition? Here are some ways that have proved effective:

   - Return the payment check, with a polite but firm statement that partial payment cannot be accepted. In many cases, this is less time-consuming than accepting payment and then entering into correspondence about the difference. A policy of this sort does take strong nerves and is not suitable for all competitive situations.
   - Submit an invoice for the discount amount immediately, explaining that late payments involve costs that you cannot afford to absorb. Or, as an alternative, the unearned discount can be added as a special item on the next regular invoice sent to the customer.
   - Eliminate the discount privilege for habitual offenders. Where this inducement to speedy payment is obviously ineffective, consider simply ending it. It is probably a good idea to point out when doing so that the company's poor payment record has caused the action, but that under better conditions the discount might be restored.

Caution

Whatever policy you follow on unearned discounts—strict or lenient—keep in mind that any nonuniform credit treatment can result in different effective prices. If your customers are in competition with each other, this can be a violation of the Robinson-Patman Act.

Unsound Practice No. 3

Indiscriminate Acceptance of Orders With Special Dating . . . on the basis of vague verbal policies:

Where top management fails to establish and enforce a formal policy's limitations and conditions, ad hoc practices soon undermine the policy. Signs of this weakness are easy to spot:

- Orders are regularly accepted without conforming to any requirement except credit approval.
- Salespeople set or agree to special terms on their own responsibility, with little or no restraint on length of terms, dollar limitations or financial strength of the customer.

The Cure

In most companies, terms of sale are considered a function of pricing, not credit, even though they may become a factor in individual credit decisions. As part of pricing, the policies governing the extension of special terms should be formulated by top management. It should establish formal guidelines to clarify company policy on these points:

- Types of accounts qualified (or unqualified) for extra terms. Example: minimal credit status and past payment experience.
- Circumstances under which the sales department should offer or acquiesce in such arrangements (competitive situations, high-profit situations and so forth).
- Limitations on length of terms extended and payment provisions.
- Norms for total extra-terms billing to all customers allowable in a given period.
- Designation of individual(s) authorized to approve orders (in compliance with policy limitations) before submissions to the credit department.

Recommendation

Even in those cases where special terms are desirable, an effort should be made to handle them on the basis of an interest-bearing note. This cannot always be done, but it is not as difficult as is sometimes supposed once the anything goes approach is no longer allowed. Even though this does not eliminate carrying the account for the longer period, it does provide some compensating advantages. It means swapping time for interest. It also sets the transaction apart in a way that connotes a significantly more binding obligation than that usually accorded an open account.

Once top management establishes the limitations, control might be delegated to sales and credit managers. Exceptions to the general policies, or conflicts between sales and credit, should be decided by top management.

Unsound Practice No. 4

Long-Term Customer Financing . . . handled under the guise of regular accounts receivable:

This practice is another offshoot of an informal, loosely controlled credit policy. It is usually indicated by:

- Accounts that are carried as non-liquidating, non-interest-bearing transactions on open-account ledger as book credit.
- Special terms that would allow customers time to resell products, obtain payment and use the proceeds for other purposes (even paying other suppliers' invoices).

While we hear a lot about customers who simply help themselves to credit concessions, not so much is said of customers who enjoy financing with the full collaboration of their suppliers. These arrangements are, as often as not, freely offered by the supplier, usually motivated by competitive necessity or the desire to secure a competitive edge. It is a practice that has been common for many years, and it is more prevalent today.

The Cure

If you find yourself in the unenviable position of financing a customer's business, re-examine your handling of long-term financing. If longer financing is deemed necessary and worthwhile, see that it is kept under sound control.

Some of the policy provisions for special terms would apply here: (1) spelling out circumstances where long-term financial applies; (2) demanding conformity with program specifications prior to submission for credit approval; and (3) setting quantitative limits, pay schedules or other conditions applicable to the individual business.

The following standard protective devices are also suggested:

- Segregated handling of long-term financing as a notes-receivable item, rather than being carried in accounts receivable with regular purchases.

Standardized agreement, integral with or supplementing an on-demand interest-bearing promissory note. The agreement should stipulate conditions under which, say, monthly installments are acceptable or the alternative on-demand provision becomes applicable. In addition, it should require, for example, periodic submission of operating results, maintenance of inventory levels and any other items pertinent to the specific arrangement.

Unsound Practice No. 5

Insufficient customer contact by credit personnel:

Under ideal circumstances, a credit manager would be in a position to contact customers to investigate credit, adjust delinquent accounts and provide financial counseling to smaller firms. Where time or other pressures prevent this, a company is likely to pay the price in the form of poor payment records, financial weakness discovered after credit was allowed or the limit raised, lack of knowledge of financial performance of major delinquencies and accounts with credit limits disproportionate to their indicated strength.

The Cure

Re-examine the possibility of stepping up personal contacts. Field travel may not be justified in all cases, such as where the typical account is too small. But where accounts run into substantial figures–particularly those whose capital investment is shared by the supplier–personal contact by credit personnel can provide advantages not available through other forms of communication. This would include the obvious advantage of mutual confidence established through personal acquaintance with customers in both day-to-day dealings and when critical situations arise.

Observation

More often that not, personal contact has been the only means of establishing credit where sufficient data might otherwise be unavailable, as well as opening up delinquent accounts for future business.

Unsound Practice No. 6

Inadequate accounts receivable reports for current needs:

Lack of complete, up-to-date accounts receivable reports makes it impossible to assess potential problems adequately and control credit and collections.

The Cure

To be effective as a control device, reports should typically provide these types of data:

- Balances carried forward from preceding periods.
- A/R trial balance, broken down by dating currently collectible and past-due accounts.
- Aged breakdown of past-due accounts.
- Changes in average collection period.
- Referrals to collection agencies for legal action and bad-debt write-offs.
- Comparison with prior periods or with budget or other objectives.

Caution

Never mistake volume for profit. Implementing the suggested cures may curtail your sales volume. If so, do not be uneasy. What you lose is probably already costing you more that it is bringing in. The last thing any business needs is volume that subtracts from the bottom line.

A Final Word

Sound credit and collection policies can improve any firm's chances of survival in difficult times and can magnify profits in good times. Unfortunately, management often does not recognize that a collection problem exists until it is too late.

Thus, even if your experience with your are accounts receivable has been satisfactory, make sure your firm maintains a sensible credit policy. The ideal time to deal with credit and collection procedures is before the storm clouds gather.

Part III

Appendices

Appendix I: Forms

Rolling 12-month forecasts are the best way to track your short-term cash flow outlook. Feel free to copy this blank form for your own use. Go to *www.encouragementpress.com* for a copy of this form. See pages 16 for details on short-term forecasting.

Rolling 12-month Forecast

	Jan.	Feb.	March	April	May	June	July	Aug.	Sept.	Oct.	Nov.	Dec.
Receipts												
Collections												
Product line A												
Product line B												
Product line C												
Product line D												
Cash Sales												
Product line A												
Product line B												
Product line C												
Product line D												
Miscellaneous												
Bank Loan(s)												

Rolling 12-month Forecast (continued)

Total Receipts												
Payments												
Suppliers												
Wages & Salaries												
Overhead												
Taxes												
Interest												
Dividends												
Debt Repayment												
Capital Items												
Total Payments												

Excess/(Deficit) ______________________

Cash Balance Beginning of Period __________

Cash Balance End of Period ______________

Forms

The following are generic forms suitable in most states. It is absolutely essential that if you chose to use these forms, that you get a legal opinion as to whether they are appropriate and legal in your jurisdiction. These forms are provided on the Encouragement Press Website by visiting *www.encouragementpress.com*.

Accounts Receivable Report

Date: ______________________________

Customer: ______________________________

Address: ______________________________

Person to Contact: ______________________________

Phone/Ext: ______________________________

Receivable on file:

____ Under 30 days ____ 30 to 60 day

____ 61 to 90 days ____ Over 90 days

Total dollar receivables: ______________________________

Allowable credit limit on receivables: ______________________________

Is customer over allowable credit limit? ______________________________

Does this client have a payment agreement? ______________________________

If so, specify: ______________________________

____

____

____

____

If no payment agreement, action to be taken: ______________________________

____

____

____

____

Bad Debt Write-Off Worksheet

Customer Account No. ______________________________

Customer Name ______________________________

Address ______________________________

____

____

Recent Purchase ______________________________

Date of Last Payment ______________________________

Balance Due ______________________________

Comments ______________________________

____

____

Write-off Requested by ______________________________

Date ______________________________

Approval Needed:

Credit Manager ______________________________

Date ______________________________

CFO/Officer ______________________________

Date ______________________________

Sales Manager ______________________________

Date ______________________________

Credit Application

Company Name: ____

Contact: ____

Address: ____

City: __________________________State: __ Zip Code: ______

Shipping Address if Different ______________________________

City: __________________________State: __ Zip Code: ______

Phone: ____

FAX: ____

E-mail: ____

Type of Business: ____

In Business Since: ____

[ ] Corporation [ ] LLC [ ] Partnership [ ] Sole Proprietor

Is a Purchase Order required? ______________________________

Authorized Buyer(s) ____

[ ] For-Profit [ ] Not-for-Profit Tax ID: ____________________

If you which to pay by credit card, please provide information below:

Credit Card Name ____

Number: ____

Exp. Date ____

Credit Application (continued)

Bank References:

____

____

____

Trade References (Please list name, address, phone number, and account number of three references. Do not list credit cards.)

____

____

____

Our terms are net 30 days. Accounts not paid in this time frame will be charged 1.5% interest rate per month and future orders will be on a C.O.D. basis until the account is current. Should collection or legal action be required to collect past dues, fees for such action will be added to your account.

Print Name: ______________________________________

Title: ____

Signed by: _______________________________________

Date: ____

Credit Approval Form

Customer Name: ______________________________

Address: ______________________________

Phone Number: ______________________________

Contact Name: ______________________________

Bank References:

____

____

____

Credit References:

____

____

____

Projected monthly income: ____________

Credit Terms: ____________ Credit Limit: ____________

Special Instructions

____

____

____

Approval signatures

Credit Manager: ____________________ Date: ________

CFO/Officer: ____________________ Date: ________

Sales Manager: ____________________ Date: ________

SECOND OVERDUE NOTICE

Date: ____________

To: ____

Our records show that as of ___________________ , ________, we have not received a response to our request for payment on your account with us, dated ___________________, ________.

If you have not yet sent payment please send a check in the amount of ____ ____________________ ($______) immediately.

If your payment has been mailed, please disregard this notice.

If your payment is not received within ten (10) working days of the date of this letter, we will take further action which may negatively affect your credit rating.

Thank you.

____

Account Representative

Final Notice

Date ____________

To: ____

RE: FINAL NOTICE BEFORE LEGAL ACTION (ACCOUNT NUMBER ____)

Dear:

I have repeatedly advised you of your long overdue balance in the amount of __________ dollars ($). Because you have not made payment I have turned your account over to my attorney with instructions to commence suit without further delay. There is still time, however, to avoid suit if you contact me within the next five (5) days.

This is be your final opportunity to resolve matters without the expense of court proceedings.

Sincerely,

Appendix II: The Resources

Books

There are a variety of publications which are worth consideration, ones that will supplement *The Business Money Book*. All of these titles are available at *www.amazon.com* and many are readily found at major book stores, particularly the larger chains. Consider the following:

The Cash Flow Management Book for Non-Profits (Jossey-Bass, 2001)

Creative Cash Flow Reporting (Wiley, 2005)–the book is actually about illegal means of misrepresenting cash flow reporting.

Consulting

Companies like CFO-Pro offer a full range of financial, consulting services. According to their Website, they typically work with medium-sized companies (no indication as to actual size in sales). For additional information, visit *www.cfo-pro.com*.

SCORE is a not-for-profit organization which partners with the Small Business Administration (SBA) to assist small and entrepreneurial companies. In addition to online advice, they have regional offices. Also, there are free forms such as a cash flow model which you can download and save in a Microsoft Office Excel worksheet. This is an excellent general resource, but also very useful for matters on cash flow, collections and credit. Visit *www.score.org* for more information.

Factoring

One of the many sites on the Web that offers help in managing cash flow through factoring (selling your accounts receivable at a discount for a third party to collect) is Eagle Capital Corporation. This company considers factoring superior to bank financing in that there is no loan to pay back and factoring is ideal for small, growing companies. For more information, visit *www.eaglecapitalcorp.com.*

While not factoring, but based on the same principle, companies who have taken personal or business notes in lieu of accounts payable may want to consider selling the notes on the open market to generate cash quicker. Naturally a percentage of the amount due is taken by the buyer of notes as their profit and to cover their risk. For information about just one of the many companies involved in this kind of business practice, visit JenseNote Investments at *www.jensennote.com.*

Professional Associations

If you are not a member, consider joining the National Association of Credit Management (NACM). In addition to the expected accreditation and certification, the NACM offers timely information, seminars, books, CDs, forms and a variety of products and services to members and non-members alike. For additional information, visit *www.nacm.org.*

An interesting site which offers advice and assistance to entrepreneurs of all stripes is the Ewing Marion Kauffman Foundation Website, called eVenturing. The material is written by entrepreneurs for entrepreneurs; there does not seem to be any cost for registering with the site and for using any of the content produced by the foundation. For further information, visit *www.eventuring.org.*

While a rather informal membership organization, readers may find Credit and Collections World an interesting and useful Website. Among the features are a salary survey for collection professionals; career postings for those interested in changing jobs; direct access to the Dunn & Bradstreet Website; a variety of white papers and special reports for collection specialists; and a listing of forthcoming conferences and meetings for industry professionals.

For additional information, visit *www.creditcollectionsworld.com.*

ACA International, the Association of Credit and Collection Professionals (ACA), is the comprehensive, knowledge-based resource for success in the credit and collection industry. Founded in 1939, ACA brings together more than 5,500 members worldwide, including third-party collection agencies, asset buyers, attorneys, creditors and vendor affiliates. ACA establishes ethical standards, produces a wide variety of products, services and publications, and articulates the values of the credit and collection industry to businesses, policymakers and consumers. As a membership organization, there are fees to join. Visit *www.acainternational.org* for more information.

Services

A number of organizations will assist with either outsourcing your credit function or offering advice from consulting services to skip tracing. Among them is Associated Credit Managers, Inc., a fee-based company which offers everything from credit scoring to credit application processing. For more information about this company, visit *www.ascmi.net.*

Most major banks, including JPMorganChase offer a variety of services that enhance the collection process and the receipt of cash from customers. Typically, everything from lockbox services to automated clearing house (ACH) payment processing. Chase is representative of many banks. For additional information, visit *www.jpmorganchase.com.*

Software

Organizations like Sungard offer financial services software, in this case, particularly their AvantGard GET PAID software component to assist in the integration and management of accounts receivable. For more information, visit *www3.sungard.com/avantgard.*

Spreadsheets

A handy concept for the start-up business, 5Star Spreadsheets offers a variety of financial spreadsheets for use in cash flow and profit and loss analysis. For more information and costs of the spreadsheets, visit *www.5starspreadsheets.com.* Remember, it beats starting from scratch if you are a new company.

Websites

AllBusiness claims to be a one-stop resource for businesses, particularly small ones. A good deal of content is available for no charge and the company claims to have one of the best sites like this in the world. (There are some annoying features, such as a company spokes person you cannot turn off when try to find out more about this company). Their services cover all aspects of business. They partner with a variety of providers, and registration is free. For more information, visit *www.allbusiness.com.*

Inc.com is useful site, with a good deal of free content in a variety of subjects for the small and growing business–its target market. Naturally, you are bombarded with advertisements and appeals to sign up for their signature magazine. Nevertheless, there is useful information to be had. Visit *www.inc.com* for details.

BizHelp24 is an English Website which also has a good deal of free content and related advertisements to entice you. While British, the basics are the same–remember to convert sterling to dollars, of course. To get more information, visit *www.bizhelp24.com.*

The Canadian government offers assistance to companies through a Website called Canada Business. One article in particular was about preparing cash flow forecast, an absolutely essential task no matter how big or small your company. For more details, visit *www.cbsc.org.*

The American Banker Online is a substantial resource Website. While the main thrust is banking and related industry news and information, there are substantial resources for those in the credit and collection industry. Visit *www.americanbanker.com* for additional details.

For those in the credit card or related industries or if you use credit cards as part of your credit granting strategy, you may find Card Forum useful and informative. The Website offers latest information from Cards&Payments (formerly Credit Card Management), ATM&Debit News, and CardLine about electronic payments, credit, debit and smart cards, card issuing, merchant acquiring, collections and recovery, card marketing, retail programs, risk management and security, economics, technology, and international card programs. For further information visit *www.cardforum.com.*

Knowing the law when it comes to collections is absolutely essential. A variety of resources are available at *www.allbusiness.com/business-finance/cash-management-collections/2976485-1.html*. There is are a variety of resources and information available at this Website. Do a bit of searching and you can gain a great deal of free information.

Credit and Collections is a 10-year-old association for professionals in the credit and debt collection industry, including credit managers, people starting a collection agency, business owners and anyone who wants to learn and network. The organization now has over 1,000 members. Among the items offered for sale are a series of books by Michelle Dunn on a variety of collection issues, including writing better collection letters, starting a collection agency and standard forms used within the industry. While it is free to be a member, you do have to link with either your e-mail address or your Website–which means that you will receive emails from vendors and others. The Members tab will bring you to a map; by clicking on your state, a variety of vendors and services in your local area are listed. For more information, visit *www.credit-and-collections.com.*

A content rich Website for all aspects of business, including credit and collection, is Business Owner's Toolkit from CCH. You can use the search box to find anything that is available on the subjects of cash flow, credit, accounts receivable, collections and more. To see what is available, visit *www.toolkit.cch.com.*

Many of the concepts explained in this book are discussed at a Website called BusinessTown.com. Everything from basic accounting to credit and collections is offered. The site is particularly good for the small businesses and newcomers to the credit and collection fields. For more information, visit *www.businesstown.com/accounting/credit.asp.*

Appendix III: Financial Ratios & Formulas

Average Collection Period

The calculation is as follows:

accounts receivable÷credit sales x 360 = average collection period

This will show how fast money is being collected–35 to 46 days is normal.

Calculating Gross Cash Flow

The formula is simple: net income plus depreciation or:

(cash flow = net income + depreciation)

The formula represents more a measurement of profitability, or what some business researchers call gross cash flow, than net cash flow.

Current Liabilities to New Worth Ratio

The simple formula is:

current liabilities÷net worth.

The lower the ratio, the better.

Current Ratio

The formula is:

current assets ÷ current liabilities = current ratio

Ideally, a current ratio of 2.0 or better indicates an acceptable margin of safety.

Days Purchases Outstanding Ratio

This ratio compares current accounts payable with annual purchases. This ratio will tell you the average time you take to pay your suppliers. The formula is as follows:

current accounts payable ÷ total annual purchases x 365 =
average # days you take to pay your suppliers

Debt Ratio

The formula is:

total liabilities÷total assets

This indicates the percentage of total assets financed by debt.

Debt/Equity Ratio

The formula is:

long-term debt (including leases)÷total assets

A lower number is optimal.

Flow-of-Funds Calculation: Accounts Payable

Use this same principle to understand accounts payable by substituting the cost of goods sold for sales. First, divide cost of goods sold for the most recent year by 365 to obtain an average day's cost of goods sold. Then divide that figure into accounts payable to obtain days payable outstanding

For example, if the cost of goods sold is $50,000 and accounts payable is $25,000, then the calculation is: $25,000÷($50,000÷365)=182.6 days.

Flow-of-Funds Calculation: Accounts Receivable

This calculation is designed to estimate the amount of time to collect accounts receivable; it is an average, and as such, some dollars will be collected sooner and some later. To do this simple calculation, you must know the normal number of days to collect receivables:

For example, if your collection time normally stands at about 27 days, you merely divide forecasted sales by 365 and then multiply by 27 to obtain projected accounts receivable. If sales are $100,000 then the calculation is: ($100,000÷365) x 27=$7,397 per day.

Inventory Turnover Ratio

The trend of your inventory turnover ratio is:

cost of goods sold ÷ inventory

This will give you valuable clues on your appropriate inventory levels. If this ratio is unusually low, your inventories are probably too high. Conversely, an abnormally high ratio indicates depleted inventories.

Profitability Ratio

The formula is:

retained earnings ÷ total assets x 1.4

The ratio gives an indication of the profitability of the company over time.

Quick Ratio (Acid-Test Ratio)

The quick ratio is:

(cash + accounts receivable)÷current liabilities

A ratio of 1 or better is a sign of financial strength.

Receivables Turnover Ratio

Another valid measure might be your receivables turnover ratio:

sales ÷ accounts receivable

The higher that ratio, the better.

Return on Assets Ratio

The formula is:

operating profits ÷ total assets x 3.3

This is your return on assets, a commonly used measure of profitability.

Return on Net Worth Ratio

The formula is:

net after tax income÷net worth

Working Capital from Operations

The working-capital formula is: c

urrent asset – current liabilities = working capital

This is used to measure cash flow. Even though working capital is expressed in dollars, it cannot be spent like cash.

Working Capital Ratio

The formula is:

working capital ÷ total assets x 1.2

Working Capital to Sales Ratio

The easiest way to keep tabs on the time lag between your cash outflow and income is by using the working capital to sales ratio. The formula is:

working capital ÷ sales

Index

A

B

C

G

H

I

J

L

M

N

O

P

R

S